37

Social History of Canada

H.V. Nelles, general editor

CAROL LEE BACCHI is a lecturer at the University of Adelaide.

Liberation Deferred? forms part of an on-going debate on the nature of 'first-wave feminism' – the turn-of-the-century woman suffrage movement. Historians have at times castigated the women of this movement for accepting and reinforcing traditional sex-role stereotypes for women. More recently, emphasis has been placed on their solid contribution to female liberation as they extended woman's domain from the domestic to the public sphere.

This book goes behind the rhetoric and politicking, to analyse the basis of the ideology of the men and women who campaigned for female enfranchisement. It focuses upon the English-speaking suffragists, looks briefly at the history of the suffrage societies, and traces their other reform affiliations in an attempt to discover who they were and why they wanted women to vote.

Bacchi finds that they belonged to an Anglo-Saxon, Protestant, well-educated elite and shared, in spite of such other diverse interests as prohibition and civic reform, a common aim: to slow down the pace of social change and reinstate Christian values in society. They felt that female enfranchisement would both add good Christian women to the electorate and double the family's representation. Unwilling to challenge the values and institutions which they perceived as necessary to social order, they limited their demands to the area of 'public housekeeping.'

CAROL LEE BACCHI

Liberation Deferred?

The Ideas of the English-Canadian
Suffragists, 1877–1918

UNIVERSITY OF TORONTO PRESS

Toronto Buffalo London

© University of Toronto Press 1983
Toronto Buffalo London
Printed in Canada

ISBN 0-8020-2455-6 cloth
ISBN 0-8020-6466-3 paper

Canadian Cataloguing in Publication Data

Bacchi, Carol Lee.
    Liberation deferred?

    (Social history of Canada, ISSN 0085-6207; 37)
    Bibliography: p.
    Includes index.
    ISBN 0-8020-2455-6 (bound). – ISBN 0-8020-6466-3 (pbk.)

    1. Women – Suffrage – Canada – History. 2. Women –
    Canada – Social conditions. I. Title. II. Series.

    JL192.B22   324.6'23'0971   C82-094588-9

36, 548

Social History of Canada 37

Acknowledgments for illustrations: Flora Macdonald Denison
Papers, Thomas Fisher Rare Book Library (Flora Macdonald
Denison and Canadian delegation to American suffrage parade);
Manitoba Archives, Events 173/3, 1915 (Manitoba Political Equality
League Petition)

Contents

Preface

Over the last fifteen years a controversy has raged within the historical community about the merits of the turn-of-the-century woman suffrage campaign.[1] The first histories, like Eleanor Flexner's *Century of Struggle* and Catherine Cleverdon's *Woman Suffrage Movement in Canada*, were mainly descriptive narratives which lauded the movement's march forward in a celebratory fashion.[2] A second, revisionist wave, headed by William O'Neill, discovered 'shortcomings' in the suffragists' attitudes and goals. Because the majority accepted the basic family structure and woman's role as 'keeper of the hearth,' they failed to live up to the feminist expectations of this group.[3]

A new revisionist school, associated with Ellen du Bois, has argued that it is unfair to judge the suffragists by contemporary standards. Du Bois points out that, in the context of the times, it took great courage to suggest that women leave their domestic sphere to assume public duties. The fact that the suffragists accepted traditional sex role stereotyping is understandable, say the new revisionists, given that they had first to overthrow the barricades constructed to keep women from any public activity, and that the whole conception of stereotyping is a relatively modern theoretical concept.[4]

Be that as it may, most historians of the movement would agree that the suffragists justified their entry into the public sphere by emphasizing the benefits to be gained from women's traditional virtues. Very few saw the need for a radical restructuring of sex roles. Few had even gone so far as to suggest that women needed to represent themselves in Parliament. Rather, the majority argued that, given the intrusions into the home in a modern industrial world, home protection required a wider sphere of action for women, the home's natural protectors. Because this line of argument helped increase the status of the home and home duties and by extension those responsible for home duties, the suffragists have been called 'domestic feminists' and 'maternal feminists.'[5] But the limitations on this type of feminism are fairly obvious. In fact it could be maintained that arguments of this nature confirmed and strengthened the view that woman's domestic virtues were her chief contribution to the world, and this in turn hindered the growth in opportunities for women in other spheres in the post-suffrage era.

For this reason, it is very important to understand why 'public housekeeping' became the limit of most suffragists' demands. In a recent article Wayne Roberts attributed the triumph of maternal feminism to the lack of participation of working women in the movement.[6] But this only tells part of the story. The key to understanding the suffragists' attitudes lies in discovering who they were and why exactly they wanted women to vote.

Canada's suffrage societies attracted both men and women, a point often overlooked. These people belonged to a well-educated Anglo-Saxon, Protestant élite composed of journalists, doctors, lawyers, educators, clerics, and a few entrepreneurs. For most, woman suffrage was only one of a series of reforms which they supported. Many were prohibitionists; many worked in Church groups; many belonged to civic reform associations.

These diverse interests, including woman suffrage itself, had a common aim, to slow down the pace of social change and to reinstate Christian values in society. The problems accompanying rapid industrialization and urbanization – the increase in crime, intemperance, and prostitution, the visible poverty and disease, the industrial unrest and social divisiveness – prompted this élite to take charge. The family ranked high in their model of an ordered society and consequently their efforts were concentrated upon raising its status. They supported female enfranchisement primarily because they believed that it would simultaneously add good Christian women to the electorate and double the family's representation. Only a small feminist minority suggested that women be freed from familial ties to allow them to pursue careers of their choice.

The suffragists therefore did not operate in a vacuum. They were members of a particular social class and the anxieties and attitudes of that class are reflected in their programme. Predictably they did not challenge values and institutions seen as absolutely necessary to their perception of the social order.

This book first took shape as a thesis completed under Professor Carman Miller's supervision at McGill University. I am ever grateful to him for his insight, encouragement, and criticism. I am also indebted to all the library and archival staff members who have assisted me over the years. I would also like to thank the typists, Pam Wilson and Beverly Arnold, for their precision and dedication to detail. My final and very personal thanks go to my friend and husband, Fred Guilhaus, for his patience and encouragement.

This book has been published with the help of a grant from the Social Science Federation of Canada, using funds provided by the Social Sciences and Humanities Research Council of Canada, and a grant from the Publications Fund of the University of Toronto Press.

Abbreviations

A of S	Archives of Saskatchewan
PAC	Public Archives of Canada
UTA	University of Toronto Archives
WLUA	Wilfrid Laurier University Archives
CSA	Canadian Suffrage Association
CWSA	Canadian Woman Suffrage Association
DWEA	Dominion Women's Enfranchisement Association
NCW	National Council of Women of Canada
NEFU	National Equal Franchise Union
Sask. PEFB	Saskatchewan Provincial Equal Franchise Board
TWLS	Toronto Women's Literary Society
UFWA	United Farm Women of Alberta
WCTU	Woman's Christian Temperance Union
WGGA	Women's Grain Growers' Association

Why Women Need the Vote

Because no race or class or sex can have its interest properly safeguarded in the Legislature of a country unless it is represented by direct suffrage.

Because women, whose special care is the home, find that questions intimately affecting the home are being settled in Parliament, where they are not represented. Such questions include housing, education, the death-rate of infants, vaccination, the employment of children, sweating, the labor of married women, unemployment, the care of the aged, and many other matters.

Because great numbers of women, who have to earn their own living, and often that of their children, find that the theory that woman is better off shielded and protected by man than in working out her own salvation has completely failed.

Because politics and economics go hand-in-hand, and while men voters can get their economic grievances attended to, non-voters are disregarded. Women are thus compelled to sell their labor cheap, and in consequence men are undercut in the labor market and the capitalist reaps the advantage.

Because women are taxed without being represented, and taxation without representation is tyranny. They have to obey the laws equally with men, and they ought to have a voice in deciding what those laws shall be.

...

Because the wisest men and women see that decisions based on the conjoined judgment of men and women are more valuable than those based on either singly.

Because so long as the majority of the women of a country have no interest in politics or in the national life, the children grow up ignorant of the meaning of the struggle for freedom, and lessons learnt in one generation by bitter experience have to be relearnt by succeeding generations.

Because, wherever women have become voters, reform has proceeded more rapidly than before.

Because women, equally with men, need interest in the larger human life outside the home, and will be better, truer women when they have a responsible interest in it.

Because the responsibility of women as citizens is essential to the establishment and development of social justice and order and to the wise and efficient government of a nation. For a nation is but a larger home. And the wide-world knows that Woman's love and judgment and voice are needed in the home.

Woman's Suffrage Headquarters
261 Yonge Street, Toronto.

Flora Macdonald Denison, president of the Canadian Suffrage Association, 1908–10, 1911–14. *Toronto World*, 16 March 1913

Canadian delegation to the American suffrage parade, Washington, on the eve of the Wilson inaugural. *Toronto World*, 16 March 1913.

Left to right, wearing banners: Flora Macdonald Denison, Harriet Dunlop Prenter, Mrs Charles MacIvor, Dr Margaret Gordon, Dr Margaret Johnston, Dr Augusta Stowe-Gullen, Constance A. Hamilton; the girl is Flora Macdonald Lapham, Mrs Denison's niece.

Presentation by the Manitoba Political Equality League of its petition, 23 December 1915.
Clockwise from top left: Lillian Beynon Thomas, Mrs F.J. Denison, Mrs Amelia Burrit (age 93), Dr Mary Crawford

LIBERATION DEFERRED?

Introduction

Compared to those of other English-speaking, industrialized communities, Canada's suffrage movement started late and success came rather easily. The first suffrage association appeared in Toronto in 1877, disguised as a Women's Literary Society. Between 1877 and 1918 some twenty-two organizations specifically committed to woman suffrage sprang up in cities across the country. The issue never attracted a groundswell of support. At its height in 1914, the movement probably had a total membership of ten thousand men and women, only 0.2 per cent of the adult population at that time. Still, by 1918 all women over twenty-one years of age had the federal vote, and most had a provincial franchise as well. Within the next few years the reluctant provinces followed the federal lead, the exception being Quebec where women were not enfranchised until 1940.[1]

The relatively easy victory was due to several factors, chiefly the moderate character of the movement, the nature of its leadership, and political opportunism. Most Canadian suffragists were social reformers and members of a social élite. They asked that women be allowed to vote in order to impress certain values upon society, Protestant morality, sobriety, and the family order. 'Women's Rights' in their view of things meant the right to serve. Very few became associated with the more radical feminist demands for complete educational and occupational equality. Politicians generally had no reason to fear such an innovation and simply waited for the appropriate moment to introduce it.

For the purposes of this study 'suffragists' have been defined as *only those men and women who became active members of Canadian suffrage associations.* It is clear that the cause attracted a wide range of supporters at different times who were content to work for female enfranchisement through other types of societies. The decision to restrict the analysis to 'overt' suffragists has several justifications. Firstly, the fact that certain men and women form or join a society publicly associated with a particular cause testifies to the degree of their commitment. Secondly, through membership lists, this group can be precisely identified. This facilitates generalizations about social composition and allows links to be drawn between woman suffrage and other reforms. Finally, the relationship between the members of declared suffrage associations and those men and women in the community who supported female enfranchisement but refused to join these associations reveals some of the stresses and strains in the Canadian social structure, particularly between the women of different classes.

It has proved difficult to identify the rank and file members of the various suffrage societies. But through newspaper reports and association minutes, their executives have all been traced, providing a sample of 156 women and 44 men. While the absence of data on the 'ordinary' membership necessarily imposes limitations on the conclusions reached in this study, the composition of the leadership still reveals a great deal about the movement. Moreover, the study of an élite is quite compatible with the study of the ideology of a movement as the élite usually formulates and propagates that ideology and usually understands the movement better than those distant from the central organizations.[2]

The leaders of the suffrage societies appear to have been quite a select group. Several indicators point to the conclusion that the movement was 'well led.' Almost 60 per cent of the female suffrage leaders were employed outside the home, a rather remarkable statistic given that in 1911 only 14.3 per cent of the total female population over age ten were gainfully employed. In the main these women were professionals – journalists, doctors, educators, with a sprinkling of lawyers and businesswomen. The housewives in the movement (some 35 per cent) had husbands who were either professionals, clerics, or businessmen. The male suffrage leaders came from the same occupational categories, with a sizeable representation of clergymen and Members of Parliament.[3]

Their educational background also testifies to their high social status. Of the 156 female leaders, 33 held an MA or better, 17 a BA, 13 had attended normal school, 12 graduated from Ladies' Colleges and Collegiate Institutes, and 5 were educated privately. Over 50 per cent of the male leaders also held university degrees.[4]

Socially, therefore, the movement, at least at the executive level, seems fairly cohesive. It attracted what may loosely be called 'middle-class' men and women, with a heavy concentration of professionals.[5] Ethnically, the executive members were similarly homogeneous, being mostly native-, British-, or American-born.[6] Their names suggest that the majority shared a common Anglo-Saxon heritage.[7] Their religious affiliations confirm this conclusion, since most were either Methodists, Presbyterians, Anglicans, or members of smaller Protestant Churches.[8]

The fact that men formed a significant proportion of the executive is important and is seldom mentioned in studies of the suffrage movement. Clearly we need to investigate their motives in order to understand the true nature of the movement. Part of the answer to this question lies in their other reform interests. Most male and female suffragists participated in a wide range of reform activities. The vast majority in fact held memberships simultaneously in suffrage societies and in reform associations dedicated to other causes. Some 25 per cent of the female suffragists and 27 per cent of the male were members of temperance societies.[9] Another 37 per cent of the female leaders participated in a number of reform-oriented associations; for example, three belonged to Charity Organization Societies, six to the Winnipeg Women's Civic League, seven to the McGill University Women's Club, four to societies for the protection of the feeble-minded, seven to child welfare associations, three to parks and playgrounds associations, seven to the Montreal Women's Club, and several to purity groups.[10] The men were equally active.[11] The types of reform which interested them can be narrowed down to

TABLE 1
Occupations, activities of suffrage leaders

	Numbers		Percentages	
	Male	Female	Male	Female
Ministers	12	–	27.3	–
Journalists, authors	4	39	9.0	25.0
Lawyers	3	1	6.8	0.6
Doctors	–	19	–	12.2
Civil servants, MPs	7	7	15.9	4.5
Educators	7	23	15.9	14.7
Businessmen	2	4	4.5	2.6
Labour reps	1	–	2.3	–
Union organizers	–	1	–	0.6
Philanthropists	1	2	2.3	1.3
Lecturers	–	2	–	1.3
Agriculturists	–	2	–	1.3
Musicians	–	1	–	0.6
Artists	–	2	–	1.3
Unknown	7	53	15.9	33.9
Total	44	156	100*	100*

* Figures do not add up to 100 because of rounding errors.

TABLE 2
Occupations of husbands of married suffragists

	Numbers	Percentages
Medicine, physicians, dentists	12	11.0
Lawyers	7	6.0
Educators	8	7.0
Journalists, publishers	4	3.6
Public servants, MPs	11	10.0
Businessmen	19	17.0
Ministers	6	5.4
Unknown	43	39.0
Total	110	100.0

TABLE 3
Religious affiliation of the suffrage élite

	Numbers		% distribution of those identified			
	Male	Female	Male	Female	Total	Canada*
Methodist	6	22	21.4	30.5	28	14.9
Presbyterian	10	13	35.7	18.0	23	15.5
Baptist	3	5	10.7	7.0	8	5.3
Anglican	3	17	10.7	23.6	20	14.5
Congregational	4	1	14.2	1.4	5	.5
Unitarian	1	3	3.5	4.2	4	–
Other Protestant	–	3	–	4.2	3	–
Roman Catholic	–	3	–	4.2	3	39.3
Agnostic	1	2	3.5	2.7	3	–
Quaker	–	2	–	2.7	2	–
Free Church	–	1	–	1.4	1	–
Unknown	16	84	–	–	–	–
Other	–	–	–	–	–	10.0
Total	44	156	100†	100†	100	100.0

* Percentage breakdown based on 1911 Census.
† Figures do not add up to 100 because of rounding errors.

several issues: temperance, child welfare, health reform, direct democracy, education, and municipal reform.

A few historians have noted previously the link between woman suffrage and other reforms. The connection between votes for women and the temperance campaign has been thoroughly investigated.[12] Recently, Terrence Morrison studied the interdependence between child welfare and what he has labelled the 'Woman's Rights' movement.[13] The diverse reform interests of the suffragists, however, suggest that beyond these links woman suffrage was one of an interrelated series of reforms supported by a remarkably homogeneous group of people. The temperance, child welfare, woman suffrage, and numerous other reform associations, in fact, frequently had overlapping memberships. The same names appear again and again in studies of these movements.[14] It could be argued on this evidence that a reform spirit characterized the age and woman suffrage attracted many infected with this spirit. Very few suffragists were not engaged in other reform activities. Seen this way, woman suffrage was one facet of a larger reform movement. And consequently the character of this larger movement needs to be understood in order for the woman suffrage campaign to be properly interpreted.

Obviously many reformers chose *not* to join suffrage societies. It is therefore important to discover why certain reformers and not others became suffragists. A degree of sex antagonism seems to have motivated the women. Given their background and their training they were angry at being denied the right to a political voice. Many, and of course this included most of the male suffragists, simply believed that this reform would speed up the implementation of other reforms. Because the suffrage societies attracted only certain reformers, they cannot be considered a microcosm of the larger reform movement. Nonetheless, the reform ideology still affected the suffragists' programme.

Generalizations about a 'reform ideology' are admittedly dangerous given the present state of the debate about the existence of a reform or so-called 'progressive' movement.[15] The general flourishing of reform groups in the late nineteenth and early twentieth centuries is undeniable. Further, the activities of the suffragists suggest that many of these reforms frequently attracted the same people and the same sort of people – members of an educated Anglo-Saxon, Protestant élite. Other studies of different parts of the reform movement confirm this characterization of its membership. Despite differences in emphasis, these studies also delineate a remarkably coherent picture of the types of social problems which inspired these people to take action.[16] Debate only becomes heated when a single psychological theorem such as 'status anxiety' is professed as an explanation for behaviour.[17]

The shift from the traditional order of village life, Wiebe's 'island communities,'[18] to a complex, impersonal, industrial urban structure represented the principal dilemma in the reformer's vision of the world. Whether he or she was disturbed primarily by the ending of a hierarchical system based on deference, by the increase in crime and delinquency, by the difficulty of finding definition in an impersonal, sprawling urban setting, or by the disappearance of values which had previously regulated social behaviour, there seems little doubt that social disintegration was the fear and social order the goal. The types of reforms advocated suggest the nature of their fears. Temperance, the Canadianizing of the foreigner, the battle against prostitution, the campaign for compulsory education, the desire to rescue delinquents – all reveal a common desire to restore a degree of control over society and chiefly over its deviants. It seems unnecessary to make this concern a 'status' one in order to understand reform behaviour.

Canada was changing at a rapid pace in these years. The whole period from 1878 onwards can be seen as one of general movement towards industrialization, consolidation, and social dislocation.[19] During the 'depression' of the 1870s and 1880s Canada maintained an annual growth rate of 4 per cent. After 1895, owing to a conjunction of favourable circumstances, the country sustained a period of economic expansion which made the earlier gains seem meagre. The completion of the Canadian Pacific Railway, the discovery of gold, the recovery of world trade, and the closing of the American frontier made Canada the last, best West and established the foundation for a transcontinental trading empire. Massive inflows of foreign capital after 1901, the coming of the wheat boom after 1902, and the beginning of the pulp and paper industry contributed to Canada's economic maturation. By 1920 Canada was indeed 'a nation transformed.'[20]

Economic growth was not an unmixed blessing, however. Several attendant developments – principally rapid urbanization, heavy foreign immigration, the consolidation of industry, and growing labour unrest – presented a rather frightening picture of a society divided and out of control. In 1880 over 75 per cent of Canada's population was rural; by 1900 this percentage had dropped to 62.5; by 1921 the urban population equalled the rural.[21] Unprepared for the influx, Canadian cities became congested, and slums, poverty, and disease became visible, social facts of life. Tuberculosis, venereal disease, and other infectious diseases spread quickly in crowded urban quarters and no class was immune from their contagion. City life encouraged drinking and prostitution and undermined religion. Family life lost its centrality as well. Statistics showed a positive correlation between city size, a decline in birth and marriage rates, and an increase in crime, delinquency, and truancy.[22]

The structure of power in the community was shifting also. Large industrial conglomerates became a fact of life and the influence they wielded, both economically and politically, caused some concern.[23] At the other end of the spectrum, labour unions began to flex their political muscles. Canadian labour had just begun to organize on any scale in the late nineteenth century, but Canadians always had the American example close to hand and saw their future in Haymarket, Homestead, and Pullman.[24] Even Canada's relative ethnic homogeneity was modified in these years. Between 1896 and World War I some two and a half million Southern and Eastern Europeans flooded into Canada. Many settled in already crowded urban quarters, compounding the dismal situation there.

This sequence of developments made the late nineteenth and early twentieth centuries a period of dramatic innovation. Those who joined the various reform associations sought to moderate the pace of change while limiting or removing the developments which disturbed them most. The reformers often expressed a hankering for the pre-urban model of society. The rural idyll appeared frequently in their rhetoric. The key to their ideology, according to Paul Boyer, was their desire to re-create a 'cohesive, organic community bound together by an enveloping web of shared moral and social values.'[25]

Many types of reform could lead to this 'organic community,' however. The problem with interpretations of progressivism to date is the attempt to impose a single programme upon the reformers. In fact, they flirted with several solutions. To simplify analysis these have been reduced to two models. The first, a more overtly coercive attempt to impose one's own values on society, found expression chiefly in anti-drink and anti-prostitution campaigns. The second model, generally a later development, proposed a more sophisticated approach to a complete reordering of society.[26] These reformers, called 'secular' in this study, saw themselves as members of a competent ruling élite who could create a cradle-to-grave blueprint for a new, better-ordered society.

Both models retained the family as a cement needed to hold the structure together. The more sophisticated branch was willing to supplant the family when it failed to function properly, and replace it with secondary institutions of socialization, chiefly the schools. But even these reformers preferred to strengthen this last remnant of the old village order. The family was more than an institution. It was a way of life, and a near hysteria, which finds echoes today, greeted its anticipated disintegration.[27] This attitude towards the family had important repercussions for the suffrage movement.

In the majority, the male and female suffragists, as members of the larger reform enterprise, shared its fears and apprehensions. They spoke with feeling about 'the problem of the city.' Their platforms ran the familiar gamut of reforms – temperance, censorship, factory legislation, compulsory education, child welfare laws. Both models of reform, the coercive and the more sophisticated, had spokesmen. And they pledged a similar devotion to the traditional family structure. Because they belonged to a social group which considered the family the key to the progress of society and the race, they did not question the conventional allocation of sex roles. They wanted to strengthen the family, not to disrupt it further.

A few feminists managed to break free of this dominant view and challenged the repressive features of family life. This minority demanded complete economic independence for women and their right to a choice of career, both before and after marriage. But these women remained isolated and unpopular. The majority of women in the movement decided to raise woman's status within acceptable channels. Since the reform ethic drew attention to the importance of the home and the family, they emphasized the mothers' contribution and demanded political recognition on these grounds.

The instigators of Canada's suffrage movement were feminists in the former sense. A hard core of such feminists who were willing to challenge the traditional structure of the family and traditional sex roles continued to operate until the final victory in 1918. But, from very early in its history, the suffrage cause attracted men and women who saw woman suffrage chiefly as a means of achieving other reforms and of strengthening the family by doubling its representation. The predominant reform ideology impressed its stamp upon the movement in this way and made 'maternal feminism' its chief and only contribution to women's status in this period.

Ideology has been defined as 'a system of ideas and judgements, explicitly stated and organized to describe, explain, justify a collectivity's situation and destiny.'[28] The collectivity may be either a social class, a political party, a nation, a social movement, or a sex. Obviously most people belong to several collectivities and the suffragists were no exception. The women in the movement belonged to a particular social and ethnic group, and the ideology connected with this collectivity clearly affected the way in which they interpreted their problems as women. It was not simply that one allegiance dominated but that they held a complex of social attitudes which had to have some coherence. That is, while as women they wanted greater recognition, as members of the social élite they had to seek that recognition in acceptable channels. Because of who they were, 'public housekeeping' became the logical limit of their demands.

1

The Making of a Suffragist

While it is impossible to determine the precise circumstances which made a woman interested in the suffrage issue, clearly the backgrounds of the female suffragists were similar in several ways. Most, almost 60 per cent, worked. All were well-to-do. The majority were well educated. Almost all had some reform connection. Each of these factors could and did encourage women to become politically active.

Among those who worked, some became suffragists because of their anger at discrimination in their pay packets or restrictions on their career ambitions, while the homebound suffragists seem to have been motivated more by their frustration with the narrowness of their domain. This frustration led many to join associations and societies which frequently introduced them to the large reform issues of the day. A sound liberal education served a similar function, broadening women's expectations and horizons and introducing them to current social and political theory.

I

As a result of Canada's immigrant past, women were at a premium throughout the period under investigation.[1] Because of their scarcity most women were able to find husbands and only a small proportion had to support themselves.[2] The problem of the 'female supernumerary' or surplus women which had plagued Britain since the beginning of the nineteenth century seemed irrelevant in Canada.[3] Yet a detailed demographic breakdown shows that Canadian cities had begun to follow the British pattern. Women congregated in the cities; in most of the major Eastern cities women actually outnumbered men.[4] Even in the West, where the proportion of men over women was generally far greater, the cities achieved a near balance between the sexes.[5] Consequently, because of the absence of adequate numbers of male partners, many women were compelled to become self-supporting. The ratio of female to male workers is invariably higher in the more urbanized, industrialized provinces.[6]

Most women either became domestic servants or worked in factories.[7] Technological innovations opened up new occupations for the women of a 'better class' who refused to consider either factory or domestic labour. The typewriter and the telephone made the field of office work available to women. The new department stores created a demand for unskilled sales personnel which women readily filled. The female white collar sector grew markedly in the decade 1911 to 1921.[8] 'Trade and Merchandising,' which included saleswomen, jumped from 11.6 to 15.9 per cent. 'Transportation,' which included a new corps of office personnel, advanced from 1.9 to 4.3 per cent. The proportion of professionals also made a dramatic leap from 15.9 to 24.2 per cent. This leap is deceptive, however, for the category 'professional' included teachers, nurses, and the office employees of professionals. In 1911 these three occupations accounted for 85 per cent of all female professionals.[9]

Women had a relatively easy time gaining admission to teaching and nursing. Both seemed respectable occupations for young single women. Neither detracted from woman's accepted role as helpmate, comforter, and instructor of the young. Economic considerations finally decided the issue in women's favour. Women worked for less and could 'justifiably' be paid less since they had only themselves to support. School Boards on limited budgets found this argument irresistible, especially after universal compulsory education created an immediate need for a large supply of teachers.

Because of their growing numbers in the profession, women quickly dominated the teachers' associations[10] and congregated to discuss their grievances. The discriminatory pay scale which gave men higher salaries for the same work predictably figured prominently at their meetings. Several teachers became suffragists over this issue. Two teachers' associations, in London and Toronto, formed independent Teachers' Suffrage Societies which ran on a programme of equal voting privileges and equal pay for equal work.

Prestige professions, law, medicine, journalism, and university teaching, proved more difficult to infiltrate. The women who tried to demolish the sex bar to these occupations faced serious opposition. This direct confrontation with sexual discrimination turned many into suffragists. A few examples will suggest their importance to the Canadian suffrage movement. Canada's best-known suffragist, Dr Emily Stowe, the founder of the original Toronto suffrage association, campaigned for and won permission for women to attend Canada's medical schools. Her daughter, Dr Augusta Stowe-Gullen, who revived the suffrage movement in 1906, was the first woman to receive her medical education entirely in Canada. Dr Amelia Yeomans, founder of Manitoba's first suffrage society in 1894, had been compelled to take her medical education in the United States. Ontario's first female lawyer, Clara Brett Martin, who after a long battle began her career in 1892, was also an outspoken suffragist. A Quebec suffragist, Annie Langstaff, failed to gain recognition from the Quebec Bar even after she had successfully completed her legal studies.[11]

II

Many suffragists who worked probably never encountered such overt discrimination. Besides, many (approximately 35 per cent) were housewives. Clearly these women had other reasons for their interest in the subject.

Industrialization revolutionized the urban homemaker's life. Technological innovations, such as the power washing machine, the vacuum cleaner, and the gasoline stove, lessened her work load and increased her leisure time. Collective concerns such as grocery stores, bakeries, and department stores had a similar effect, eliminating the need for a woman to can her own fruits and vegetables, bake her own bread, or make her family's clothing. The majority of the suffragists belonged to a class which could afford these innovations, and the leisure they created was clearly necessary to allow family women to participate in activities outside the home. But industrialization also had a less fortunate side-effect. It seemed to reduce the complexity and hence the importance of the woman's domestic function. One British Columbia suffragist condemned housekeeping as 'dull, unpleasant drudgery.'[12] Another, in Montreal, argued that a man would rather be dead than be tied to a 'pack of kids' and a kitchen.[13]

Partly, the problem was a status one. Contrary to the euphemistic image of women as 'Queens in their homes,' women discovered that the occupation 'housewife' possessed no official recognition in the census, required no special training, and received no remuneration. A woman might work all day at her 'calling' only to have to request pocket money from her husband in the evening.[14] Because of the low status accorded their domestic function, many women looked for activities which would win them greater respect. An idealistic philosophy which demanded that each individual somehow contribute to the progress of the race dominated the late nineteenth century.[15] This idealism moved women as well as men and some women reacted by condemning the frivolity and uselessness of the domestic routine. Dr Elizabeth Smith-Shortt, an Ottawa suffragist, for example, revealed a deep discontent in her diary with what she called her 'shallow life.' She was preoccupied with becoming 'a woman with a purpose.'[16]

The many women's organizations which proliferated in these years, including the suffrage societies, profited from this desire to break into the larger domain of public politics. Many of these societies paralleled male associations and reflected a more general feeling of individual impotency which accompanied rapid industrial growth and the spawning of collective enterprises.[17] The clubs covered a wide range of interests, artistic, literary, patriotic, religious, and reform. Some more than others played an important role in educating women socially and politically.

The Woman's Christian Temperance Union, one of the largest and most influential reform societies, started in Canada in 1873 by Letitia Youmans of Picton, Ontario, campaigned primarily for prohibition. By the turn of the century Canada had locals in most major cities and towns, provincial organizations in Quebec, Ontario, Nova Scotia, New Brunswick, Prince Edward Island, and the North West Territories, and a membership of over six thousand. Most WCTU locals had a Franchise Department dedicated specifically to the goal of woman suffrage. The frustration of campaigning annually for prohibition and being unable to do anything to see it enforced convinced some WCTU members to join outright suffrage societies. Moreover, many temperance men became suffragists because they believed that the majority of women would vote in favour of prohibition.[18]

The National Council of Women of Canada, inaugurated in 1893 under the presidency of Lady Ishbel Aberdeen, the wife of Canada's Governor-General, acted as a clearing house for the social and moral issues of the day. In an attempt to appeal to all Canadian women, the Council decided to disassociate itself from potentially divisive topics such as temperance and woman suffrage. The structure of the Council,[19] however, allowed the suffragists to infiltrate and slowly to whittle away the prejudice against their cause. At the same time many National Council members became disgruntled at their inability to help create the legislation they favoured. In 1910 the NCW, finally and reluctantly, by a vote of 71 to 51, passed a resolution endorsing female enfranchisement.[20]

Frequently, women's organizations from other countries, particularly from the United States, played a role in the political awakening of Canadian women. Both the WCTU and the NCW had their origins in the United States and were brought to Canada by women who attended American meetings. Sometimes Canada played host to visitors from the United States and overseas. On two occasions, for example, an American group, the Association for the Advancement of Women, staged conventions on Canadian soil, one in 1890 in Toronto, the second in 1896 in Saint John, New Brunswick. Both meetings received wide and favourable press coverage. American suffrage notables Julia Ward Howe, Dr Maria Mitchell, Mary F. Eastman, Lucy Stone, Martha Strickland, and Alice Stone Blackwell spoke at the Toronto gathering and undoubtedly inspired some members of the audience, which on this occasion included at least three active Canadian suffragists, Ada Mareau Hughes, Dr Susanna Boyle, and Dr Emily Stowe.[21]

Reform associations also functioned at the local level. The Montreal Women's Club, founded in 1891 by a prominent Montreal woman, Mrs Robert Reid, and modelled on the Chicago Women's Club, is but one example. This society also served as a political educator. The members discussed numerous women's and more general social problems, including women's legal position in Quebec, the status of women in the academic professions, prison reform, and new methods of education.[22] Not surprisingly, several members later became Montreal's leading suffragists – Dr Grace Ritchie, Carrie Derick, Helen R.Y. Reid, Margaret Polson Clark Murray, and Henrietta Muir Edwards.[23]

Patriotic associations like the Women's Canadian Club and the Imperial Order of Daughters of the Empire strengthened women's nationalist commitment. Business associations such as the Canadian Business Women's Club, the Canadian Women's Press Club, and the many Teachers' Associations provided a forum where common grievances could be discussed. Civic clubs, social science clubs, and consumer protection leagues emphasized current social problems and the need for greater state interference. Religious societies brought women into touch with the new social gospel. Each, whether overtly political or not, served essentially the same function, drawing women out of the confines of their homes and encouraging them to think, to discuss, and to question.

III

Education seems to have been the single most important factor which converted women to 'suffragism.' It provides a common denominator for the entire membership. The vast majority, early and late, were well educated. Of those identified, over 57 per cent had attended a regular university while another 30 per cent graduated from Normal Schools or Ladies' Colleges and 6 per cent were educated privately.[24]

Paradoxically, the initial expansion of educational opportunities for women was not intended to produce dissent. In fact, it was to have had quite the reverse effect. Many clergy and well-to-do citizens promoted a higher education for women because they feared that the existing schools encouraged young women to be flighty and frivolous. Moved by the impulse to re-establish a strict moral order, they became convinced that the mothers of the next generation needed greater 'mental discipline' in order to handle capably the moral instruction of the young. Moreover, it had become obvious that many young women, unable to find suitable mates, had to work to support themselves or be forced to resort to less honourable means. For both these reasons, higher education for women became a very respectable cause in late-nineteenth-century Canada.

New academies were opened, many of which were simply finishing schools while others provided a more challenging curriculum.[25] A second innovation, Women's Education Associations, offered college-level courses, in conjunction with a leading university, to well-to-do young ladies.[26] While these Associations promoted 'general culture' rather than 'professional education' for women, they at least made it acceptable for women to display some evidence of intelligence.

The next logical development, the opening of colleges to women, took one of three forms in the English-speaking world. The United States promoted the all-female college of the Vassar or the Sophia Smith variety; Britain on the other hand favoured the Co-ordinate College, a separate institution with separate facilities, but directly associated with a male university.[27] A third alternative, popular for economic reasons in Britain and America, allowed women to take their courses side by side with the men in coeducational institutions. Most Canadian universities chose the third option and permitted women to enrol alongside the men. The Maritime provinces lowered the sex barrier first, Mount Allison admitting women in 1862, Acadia in 1880, and Dalhousie in 1881. In Ontario, Queen's University accepted women in 1872 and Victoria College of Cobourg in 1877.[28]

Where economically viable, however, Canadian educators preferred the British Co-ordinate College. In 1883 Donald Smith created an endowment for the construction of a Woman's College adjacent to McGill, dependent upon the 'maintenance of separate classes for women.' Despite the opposition of McGill's redoutable Professor of Philosophy, John Clark Murray, a champion of equal educational opportunities for women, the policy of 'separate but equal' stood and Royal Victoria College opened its doors to Montreal women in 1901.[29] In Ontario in 1884 the Principal of the University of Toronto, Sir Daniel Wilson, responding to pressure that he admit women to the University, wrote the Minister of Education, requesting a separate college for women. The Ontario Legislature, however, had no Smith endowment to fall back upon and therefore reluctantly granted women permission to study alongside the men.

While the quality of women's education improved, the curriculum remained tailored to produce wives and mothers. Women could study Moral Philosophy, Religion, Literature, and Languages, subjects designed to broaden their minds, but courses which trained them to become self-supporting, thereby encouraging them to abandon the home, were considered both wrong-minded and dangerous. Higher education for women aimed at strengthening not undermining the family. Even Clark Murray himself argued that the importance of woman's role *within* the family necessitated her education: 'Those who had most at heart the importance and sacredness of the family as the centre of all that was best in humanity felt most strongly that no education was too high for her whose influence in the family was most potent ...'[30]

As a result of these attitudes, access to professional education came much more slowly, with teaching, of course, remaining the exception. Canada's first doctors had to take their degrees in American universities.[31] Eventually, under pressure, Women's Medical Colleges were established in 1883 in Kingston and Toronto. The idea of a 'Women's' Medical College seemed more respectable to Victorians, who felt it indiscreet for men and women to study the body, particularly the male body, together. But economics and low enrolment made segregation impractical and in 1906 the University of Toronto absorbed the women's section. Smaller institutions such as Dalhousie found it more practical to admit women to its Medical Faculty from its founding in 1881. Admission to professional training counted only one step in the road to professional equality, however. Hospitals in Montreal, for example, refused to allow women to practise in their clinics, forcing Bishop's College to close its doors to female medical students in 1900. The same applied to law. Although few universities objected to women taking legal studies, the Bars refused them the right to practise.

Educators who had intended that more advanced studies only develop a woman's mental discipline, fitting her better for her maternal duty, underestimated the effects of education. Many intelligent women, after attending college, became restless and sought more fulfilling work than the traditional domestic routine. Higher education began an irreversible process which led women to demand access to the world outside the home. Many women who took their first training in Normal Schools aspired after more education and more challenging career opportunities. Several suffragists who began their lives as teachers went on to become doctors or journalists.[32]

Moreover, the type of education the women received produced an activist frame of mind. In Moral Philosophy and in Literature they were introduced to the great social ideas of the age. The McGill curriculum, for example, included readings on William Morris' *Social Theories*, the reports of Toynbee Hall, and Benjamin Kidd's *Social Evolution*. The spirit of social reform infected the classroom. According to one historian, practical idealism replaced religion as the creed of late-nineteenth-century man.[33] The humanists T.H. Huxley, T.H. Green, and Kidd, men who attempted to civilize the Darwinian struggle for existence, came into vogue. The message of the era was '"Usefulness", "social reform", the bettering of daily life for the many ...'[34] Women could no more read Charles Booth's *Life and Labour of the People in London* or Seebohm Rowntree's *Poverty: A Study of Town Life* and remain unmoved than could their husbands, brothers, and fathers. Many revolted against the complacent, inactive, useless life of traditional middle-class wifedom and demanded an arena for action. In the words of Carrie Derick, a prominent Montreal suffragist, they wanted 'to do,' to put what they had learned into practice. In the first glow of their political awakening, in 1891, the McGill Women's Alumnae opened a Girls' Club and Lunchroom, the forerunner of the McGill University Settlement.[35] Political consciousness followed closely upon an awareness of social issues, and many women came to be suffragists through this channel.

In an even more direct manner, college life introduced women to the woman's movement. Following the male example, female students formed debating and alumnae societies. At their meetings the women naturally discussed topics of current public and political interest, touching inevitably on the so-called 'woman's question.' In 1896 the McGill Alumnae staged debates on 'The Present Course for Women at McGill,' 'The Advisability of Women Working for Money,' and 'Woman's Duty in Municipal Matters.'[36] Encouraged by the progress women had made, impressed particularly by their own promotion into the intelligentsia, it is not surprising that many decided that they ought to possess a vote.

The suffrage movement profited from the opportunities made available to women in the late nineteenth century. In fact, it could not have emerged *but* for these developments. The sex ratio in the city and the new jobs made available by technological change drew women into the labour market. It became necessary and acceptable for women to work. Independent-minded women naturally began to question the restrictions placed on the type of work available to them. Those who remained housewives took advantage of the leisure created by new domestic innovations to participate in extra-familial activities. Urban congestion and the new industrialism evoked a reform movement which touched both men and women. Women encountered the new social ideas in college and in reform associations. The heavy emphasis on individual activism and government intervention led many to seek the franchise. The whole idea of a liberated womanhood emerged as a consequence of industrialization and its social repercussions: women may have felt stifled by the restraints of the nuclear family and dull, domestic routine in pre-industrial times,[37] but industrialism compounded the sensation of uselessness and powerlessness at the same time as it offered women opportunities to break out of the routine by either taking a job, going to school, or joining some society.

2

Suffrage Organization in Canada: Feminism and Social Reform

The suffrage movement in Canada was launched by women with a strong feminist commitment, frequently the same moving spirits who tried to batter down the sexual barriers constructed to keep women from prestige occupations. These women challenged the sexual division of labour and even suggested that married women had a right to work, a radical innovation in this period. This feminist clique, centred in Toronto, created a network of hard-core activists who provided organizational leadership and who revived interest when the movement lapsed into despondency. Because of the unpopularity of their views, they remained an ideological and numerical minority.

From very early in the movement's history, men and women with a prior interest in reform and a moderate social philosophy began to flood into the suffrage societies. Many of these women at times demonstrated a degree of sex antagonism, but they proved unwilling to demand serious changes in the social structure. They were social reformers first and this made them staunch supporters of the traditional family. Similarly the male reformers were social conservatives who supported votes for women because they wanted good Christian womanhood to have a political voice. They envisioned no real change in sex roles. The reform ethos captured the suffrage movement and transformed it into a defender of the social status quo.

Instead of the two-wave pattern discovered in the American suffrage movement by Aileen Kraditor, in which a feminist first wave was supplanted by a social reform wave,[1] Canada's two suffrage branches operated in tandem. Perhaps this was because of the comparatively late interest in the subject in Canada. By the time feminist stirrings had concrete expression in suffrage societies (Canadian women did not have the experience of the anti-slavery battle which created America's first feminists),[2] the social conditions which produced the reform movement – the growth of industry and the appearance of urban slums – already existed. Hence, even Canada's first suffrage societies quickly acquired this dual, feminist/social reform character, with the social reformers firmly in control.

I

Emily Stowe, born Emily Howard Jennings in 1832 in Norwich, Ontario, is considered the founder of the suffrage movement in Canada. Her early education at the hands of her mother, Hannah Howard, a Quaker from Rhode Island, possibly sparked a feminist consciousness: the Quakers were well known for their egalitarian ideas towards women.[3] The eldest of six girls, Emily began teaching at age fifteen. She graduated from the Normal School for Upper Canada College in 1853 and became, at twenty, Canada's first woman principal. Four years later she abandoned her career to marry a carriage-maker, John Stowe. The Stowes had three children, two sons, John and Frank, and a daughter, Augusta. In 1864 her husband developed tuberculosis and Emily became the family's breadwinner.[4]

Following the example of two younger sisters, Emily decided to become a doctor. She encountered firsthand the opposition to women in medicine. Rejected by the University of Toronto Medical Faculty, she enrolled in the New York Medical College for Women. The experience politicized her. She met Elizabeth Cady Stanton and Susan B. Anthony, the notable American feminists, at the College and returned to Canada in 1868 a doctor and a feminist herself.[5]

Immediately Dr Stowe initiated a series of lectures on the subject of 'Woman's Sphere,' sponsored by the Mechanics' Institutes in Toronto, Oshawa, Whitby, and Brantford. The American example again stimulated her. In 1877, she attended a meeting of the American Association for the Advancement of Women and returned to establish the Toronto Women's Literary Society (TWLS). Ostensibly a society for the development of women's intellectual interests, the Toronto group was really a front for suffrage activity. In 1883, it dropped its disguise and emerged as Canada's first national suffrage association.

Dr Stowe's attitudes towards woman's sphere were advanced for her time. Many people had begun to criticize the traditional education in needlepoint and dancing available for women and suggested that women could profit from the more demanding arts curriculum. But Dr Stowe went further than this. She defended woman's right to a solid and thorough training 'in the vigorous branches of classical and mathematical science.' Moreover, she proclaimed that professional education ought to lead to professional employment. She considered the 'home circle' too narrow and too confining to absorb all of a woman's capabilities and argued that every woman ought to be free to elect for herself the employment best suited to her.[6] Dr Stowe put this belief into practice by dedicating her life to opening the study of medicine to Canadian women. She campaigned for and helped to establish the Toronto Women's Medical College in 1883. That same year, she enjoyed a sweet revenge as her daughter, Augusta Stowe-Gullen, graduated from Victoria University, the first woman to receive her medical education entirely in Canada.

Despite Dr Stowe's obvious feminist inspiration, the TWLS attracted other women whose motives are much more ambiguous. Another founding member, Sarah A. Curzon, an English-born author and playwright, had been forced like Dr Stowe to become self-supporting, following her husband's death in 1878. This fact and the subject of her most famous work, Laura Secord, one of Canada's pioneer heroines, suggest an independence of attitude that might have been feminist. But Mrs Curzon also contributed a column to *Canada Citizen*, Canada's first prohibitionist paper, revealing an early link between temperance and woman suffrage.[7] A third member, Mary McDonnell, the wife of Donald Aeneas McDonnell, soldier, politician, and public servant,[8] also had close ties with the temperance movement. A member of the incorporating committee of the Toronto Woman's Christian Temperance Union, she also headed the Dominion WCTU for several years.[9] Clearly, without diaries or more detailed biographical material, it is difficult to attribute a single character to the TWLS.

Similarly, the early suffrage societies in the other provinces seemed to spring from a variety of motives. Other than Ontario, only Nova Scotia, New Brunswick, and Manitoba had recognized suffrage societies before the turn of the century. The WCTU managed the campaign in British Columbia until that time, when several of its members became important suffrage leaders.[10] In Quebec, two associations, the Montreal Local Council of Women and the Montreal Women's Club, served as incubators for the movement.

In Nova Scotia, in 1895, a well-known novelist, Anna H. Leonowens, and Nova Scotia's first woman professor, Eliza Ritchie, organized the Halifax Suffrage Association, continuing the tradition of professional leadership.[11] The prohibitionist cause was strong in Canada's eastern provinces, however, and the WCTU had been actively campaigning for woman suffrage before the inception of this association. Between 1892 and 1895 the Nova Scotia WCTU presented thirty-four petitions on behalf of woman suffrage.[12] These temperance women formed a large part of the membership of the new suffrage society.[13] In its own right woman suffrage proved unable to maintain public interest and the society disbanded after a year, to resurface only in 1915.

New Brunswick profited from the intervention of the Toronto suffragists. As early as 1894, Sarah Curzon reported that 'down in St. John, New Brunswick, two Conservative ladies are taking the question up and that through my influence.'[14] More encouragement in 1894 resulted in the formation of the Saint John Suffrage Association, a short-lived group which disbanded in 1902. The Secretary-Treasurer of the Association for these years was Ella B.M. Hatheway, part of a husband and wife reform team which campaigned for such diverse causes as a graduated income tax, 'profit sharing,' factory legislation, and workmen's compensation.[15]

The only other pre-1900 suffrage society in Canada appeared in Manitoba. A unique group of Icelandic suffragists, led by

Margaret Benedictssen, had campaigned for woman suffrage from their arrival in the 1870s.[16] Then in 1894, Amelia Yeomans, a former Montreal woman and a medical graduate from Ann Arbor, Michigan, started up an English-speaking society, the Manitoba Equal Suffrage Club. Dr Yeomans belonged to the Manitoba WCTU, which had campaigned for woman suffrage from the 1880s. But she felt that woman suffrage had to stand on its 'sole merits.' She even feared that a temperance connection might harm the suffrage movement, driving away potential supporters who had no sympathy for prohibition.

This deliberate separation of the temperance and suffrage issues and the fact that, like Emily Stowe, Dr Yeomans had been forced to take her medical education in the United States[17] suggest that her determination to fight for woman suffrage had feminist origins. If this is so, Dr Yeomans was definitely ahead of her time, for 'on its sole merits' the Suffrage Club lasted but one year. Many more people in Manitoba, it seems, approved of woman suffrage as the means to another end, prohibition.

The same was true in Toronto where the Canadian Woman Suffrage Association (CWSA), the successor to the TWLS, began to attract men and women with wide reform interests. The association had forty-six male and forty-nine female members in 1883 and an executive of seven men and twelve women. On the executive sat William Houston, President of the University of Toronto Political Science Association, a leading advocate of municipal reform and a public school inspector; T. Phillips Thompson, a prominent Labour reformer and Secretary and organizer of the Ontario Socialist League; and John Hallam, a merchant and ex-alderman, labelled a 'radical of the Lancashire type' for his support of free trade and opposition to direct taxation.[18] The rank and file included such notables as the Honourable George Eulas Foster, called by Frances Willard the 'Neal Dow' of Canada, and Robert Jaffray, president of the Toronto Reform Association.[19]

The female members also demonstrated a more conspicuous social reform alliance. The well-known philanthropist and founder of Moulton Ladies' College, Susan McMaster, joined the executive in 1883, as did Mrs J.W. Bengough, wife of the cartoonist and prohibitionist John W. Bengough.[20] Margaret Carlyle, a businesswoman and an inspector of factories, Jennie Gray Wildman, a staff member of the Ontario Women's Medical College and an organizer of the Canadian Purity Education Association, and Minnie Phelps, a member of the Grand Templars and Corresponding Secretary for the Ontario WCTU, also joined the CWSA.[21]

The suffrage movement languished between 1884 and 1889. Perhaps the diffuse reform interests of its new members distracted the CWSA from its original purpose. Emily Stowe explicitly blamed the men for the lull in activity: 'The truth of the matter is we admitted the opposite sex as members and the effect was demoralising. That old idea of female dependence crept in and the ladies began to rely upon the gentlemen rather than upon their own efforts.'[22]

In 1889 Dr Stowe and her daughter attempted to revitalize the movement. They brought to Toronto a select group of American suffragists, Anna Howard Shaw, Susan B. Anthony, and May S. Howell, to launch the new Dominion Women's Enfranchisement Association, and hired Mrs Howell as a paid organizer.[23] The DWEA had some successes. It established branch societies in nearby communities and as far afield as Saint John, New Brunswick. On its recommendation, Toronto's Mayor, Edward Frederick Clarke, invited the American Association for the Advancement of Women to hold its Eighteenth Annual Congress in the city, attracting considerable publicity. Three DWEA members, Augusta Stowe-Gullen, Mary McDonnell, and Mrs A. Vance, contested seats on the Toronto School Board in 1892, and both Dr Stowe-Gullen and Mrs McDonnell were elected.[24] In 1896, the DWEA staged a Mock Parliament, the first of its kind in Canada, involving over fifty women.

Despite these efforts, the dilution of the movement by reformers with different motives and different priorities continued. Dr Stowe tried in vain to regain the leadership of the movement for women; but the final defeat of her efforts came in 1891 with the appointment of the well-known education reformer, James L. Hughes, to the presidency of the central Toronto Suffrage Club.[25] Many other male reformers and an ever-increasing number of temperance women joined the DWEA.[26] At the 1889 organizational meeting, Mrs Jacob Spence, mother of the veteran pro-hibitionist F.S. Spence, Annie Parker, Superintendent of the Dominion WCTU in 1891, and Mrs D.V. Lucas, the wife of Rev Daniel Vannorman Lucas, an active prohibitionist in Australia and in Ontario, dominated the platform party.[27] In the 1896 Mock Parliament, Annie O. Rutherford, WCTU President for many years, held the honoured position of Speaker.[28] Other well-known temperance women occupied seats on both sides of the House.[29]

Woman suffrage was still not quite acceptable socially, although it had begun to attract a wider audience. As late as 1893 the National Council of Women deliberately disassociated itself from the original American National Council because the latter was too closely associated with the suffragists.[30] Lady Aberdeen felt it necessary again and again to reassure Canadian men that their women were not 'fanatics,' that they had no intention of march-ing into man's territory 'to rob and pillage and destroy.'[31] Only in 1910 had the suffrage issue become sufficiently innocuous for the Canadian National Council to sanction it.

In 1895 the suffrage movement stood in a no-man's-land. The few feminist founders were old and tired. The vast majority of women were unconcerned or unconverted. The 'middle men,' temperance and other reformers, placed greater emphasis on their own particular interests and began to mould woman suf-frage to suit their more moderate intentions. The second phase of Canadian suffrage history completed this task.

II

As at its instigation the rebirth of the suffrage campaign was due almost entirely to the dedication of a few feminists. In 1906 Emily Stowe's hand-picked successor, Augusta Stowe-Gullen, tried to revive interest by yet another name change. The ponder-ous Dominion Women's Enfranchisement Association became the Canadian Suffrage Association (CSA). Dr Stowe-Gullen also managed to conscript two new aggressive and energetic leaders, Flora Macdonald Denison and Margaret Blair Gordon.

These women became the core and character of the suffrage revival. All three fell firmly within the feminist tradition established by Dr Stowe. Each had battled societal prejudice to win acceptance in her chosen field. Dr Stowe-Gullen confronted and defeated the opponents of women's medical education in Canada. Margaret Gordon belonged to this same group of pioneer female practitioners, having received her medical degree from Trinity (University of Toronto) in 1898.[32] Flora Macdonald Denison was a self-made businesswoman. She had begun her career as a costumer in the Robert Simpson Company and had worked her way up to become owner of her own fashion establishment and a part-time real estate broker.[33]

The three were outspoken defenders of women's rights. Mrs Denison advocated complete economic independence for both married and unmarried women, arguing that 'The sphere of woman is only limited by her capabilities ...' and again 'Labour is not defined by gender and washing dishes is no more feminine than the sending of a marconigram is masculine.'[34] She felt that the institution of marriage robbed a woman of her individuality and reduced her to the level of a prostitute. The whole idea of signing a contract to love repulsed Mrs Denison who, perhaps not coincidentally, was in 1914 in the process of securing a divorce. Both she and Dr Gordon wished to see the word 'obey' deleted from the marriage ceremony because of the insidious implications it carried for women.[35]

Under the direction of this triumvirate, the CSA created affiliates in Saint John, Victoria, Winnipeg, and Montreal, and five new societies in Toronto. Despite these successes, the movement made little real headway until 1910 when two quite contradictory factors combined to change the whole tone and tempo of the campaign. First, the sensationalist tactics adopted by the militant British 'suffragettes' aroused the Canadian public. Second and more important, the National Council passed a resolution in favour of woman suffrage, giving the issue a new respectability. After this date, suffrage societies proliferated across the country. Important new societies included the Manitoba Political Equal Franchise League, started in 1912, the Montreal Suffrage Association, started the year following, and the Saskatchewan Provincial Equal Franchise Board, started in 1915. By 1916 Toronto alone claimed eight suffrage associations.

The movement now attracted a broader clientele. Journalists, doctors, and teachers, women who worked in a man's world, continued to play leading roles. But, thanks to the National Council's stamp of approval, the numbers of married, well-educated but non-professional women increased also. Even people of social standing, like Lady Grace Julia Drummond, philanthropist, social reformer, and wife of the Montreal Senator Hon George A. Drummond, could now give the movement their blessing. Lady Drummond became Honorary President of the Montreal Suffrage Association.[36]

The tone of the movement changed also. The new suffragists were almost unanimously social reformers first, as is indicated by this interview with one of the newcomers, Mrs A.M. Huestis, President of Toronto's Local Council of Women. Mrs Huestis outlined a long list of reforms the Local Council had prepared for the Legislature: separate trials for women, examination of female prisoners by women doctors, policewomen to deal with prostitutes, prohibition of night labour for children fourteen years of age and under, adequate segregation and care of the feeble-minded, and a housing commission to deal with the increased numbers of immigrants. When asked if she and the Council supported woman suffrage, she answered, 'Yes but that is the last plank on our platform. We put the reforms first.'[37]

The question was not simply the ranking of the suffrage. This only symbolized the new recruits' more moderate philosophy, for the majority accepted the maxim that a woman's first duty lay within the home. James Hughes, typical of the male reformers who flooded into the suffrage societies, accepted female enfranchisement because, as he saw it, a woman could obviously vote without neglecting her children for any length of time. As for electioneering and sitting in Parliament, he saw plenty of 'unmarried women and widows, and married women with grown-up children to do that.'[38] Even a suffragist as prominent as Nellie McClung, a temperance woman and a good representative of the social reform wave, could recommend careers only to

women with grown-up children, women who had already ful-
filled their maternal responsibility. After all, she explained, children do grow up, and 'the strong, active, virile woman of fifty,
with twenty good years ahead of her ... is a force to be reckoned
with in the uplift of the world.'[39] Sonia Leathes, a late-comer to
the movement in Toronto, agreed that 'the place of these women
who are wives and mothers and who have husbands who can
and will support them and their children' will certainly be the
home.[40]

Why the vote then? Simply, answered the social reform suffragist, because society through industrialization had intruded
into woman's sphere. The home had become a beleaguered for-
tress against crime, immorality, and disease. How better to
strengthen it than to allow woman, its natural protector and
guardian, a say in controlling the forces which threatened it!
'The greatest safeguard from incursions from without,' according to Elizabeth Smith-Shortt, a late convert to woman suffrage,
is 'to strengthen the forces within.'[41] Giving the vote to women,
especially to married women, increased the weight of the family
vote and so of the solid, stable element in political life.

In the hands of the social reformers, 'home protection' became
the slogan and symbol of the movement, destroying in the public
mind the association between female enfranchisement and social
revolution. They even managed to confine their political interest
to matters peculiarly feminine, to civic cleanliness, the city beautiful, education, civic morality, the protection of children from
immoral influences, the reform of delinquent children, child
labour, infant mortality, food adulteration, and public health.
All, they claimed, were legitimately 'within the province of
motherhood.'[42] Voting meant housekeeping on a municipal,
provincial, or federal level, nothing more.

Even the feminists when set on the defensive or perhaps for
tactical reasons modified their stance on sex roles. Flora Macdonald Denison in one of her weaker moments actually conceded that 'the primal mission of woman is to get married and
have children.'[43] This, of course, may have been rhetoric. With
some exceptions, historians are generally confined to public
statements of policy. But the consistency with which the new

suffragists not only accepted but eulogized woman's domestic duties suggests that they genuinely believed in the sexual division of labour. In their hands the movement became less aggressive, more conciliatory, and infinitely more popular.

III

Given the temperate nature of the suffrage majority, it is not surprising that the British militants attracted few supporters in Canada. Only the few feminist members like Dr Stowe-Gullen and Mrs Denison expressed admiration for their British colleagues' daring. The CSA at their instigation, recorded a 'hearty appreciation of the intelligence, courage and energy shown by the W.S.P.U. [Women's Social and Political Union].'[44] In 1909 the association sponsored a speaking tour by the elder Pankhurst, and in 1913 Mrs Denison spoke against the Cat and Mouse Act in a London (England) demonstration and actually joined the WSPU.[45]

In general, Canadian tactics were cautious and undemonstrative, in keeping with the country's reputed character. Canadian suffragists staged mock parliaments, sponsored plays, arranged exhibits, sold postcards, and generally used more subtle methods of persuasion. Taking the politicians at their word, that Canadian women had only to demonstrate that they wanted the vote in order to receive it, they considered the petition their most effective tool. A 1909 petition to the Ontario Premier, J.P. Whitney, contained over one hundred thousand signatures. The petition which preceded the provincial enfranchisement of Manitoba women in 1915 contained 39,584 names.[46]

With but one exception, Canadians failed to resort to anything even as tame as a march or a demonstration on their own soil.[47] A few more enthusiastic women, tired of Canadian lethargy, joined in demonstrations in other countries. Some suffragists seem to have had the money to criss-cross the Atlantic Ocean and the North American continent at will. One Toronto suffragist, Alice Chown, and a group of her friends formed an ad hoc Canadian deputation in a militant London march, each carrying a stem of wheat to identify their native land.[48] In 1913 the CSA sent a delegation to a large American demonstration on the eve of the Wilson inaugural. Still cautious, the women refused to consider using such tactics at home.[49]

Several reasons explain the Canadian women's timidity. The movement was still young and had not faced the long years of rebuke and ridicule which enraged British women. Moreover, Canadians had a reputation to uphold as non-violent, law-abiding citizens. More significantly, the movement lacked the cohesiveness and strength necessary for a concerted drive. The associations were widely dispersed and poorly organized, fragmented both by geography and ideology. Sectionalism, a problem for most Canadian social movements, troubled the suffragists as well. Although the CSA claimed national status, in fact, it had few affiliates and even less control outside of Toronto. Suffragists in British Columbia considered themselves autonomous. Suffragists in Saskatchewan, Manitoba, and Alberta co-operated with one another but wanted nothing to do with a national association directed by Eastern women. The Montreal Suffrage Association became a CSA affiliate but it too conducted its own campaign with little guidance from Toronto. With the exception of occasional encouragement to New Brunswick, the CSA also had little to do with the Maritime provinces where the WCTU led the campaigning.

More serious still were the ideological disputes within the movement. Disagreement existed primarily between the 'Old Guard' of the CSA and the new social reform suffragists. The 'Old Guard,' Dr Stowe-Gullen and her associates, supported by a few sympathizers outside Toronto – for example, the Montreal journalist Agnes Chesley, Francis Marion Beynon, editor of the Women's Section in the *Grain Growers' Guide*, and Helena Gutteridge, the British Columbia labour leader[50] – continued to raise feminist issues. They criticized marriage, questioned the motherhood role, and demanded equal educational and occupational opportunities. The social reform suffragists, on the other hand, were intent on preserving the traditional allocation of sex roles. For the feminists, the ballot symbolized a desire to change the male's conception of woman and her function. For the social reformers, woman suffrage provided the means to implement their larger reform programme and to give woman's maternal influence a wider sphere of action. The feminists invariably drew their strength from among the self-supporting women. The social reform suffragists included many working women who decided that the most pressing problems were social not sexual, and a large number of housewives for whom the problem of sexual discrimination was more remote.

These ideological disagreements resulted in an organizational split in 1914. The Toronto Equal Franchise League, headed by Constance Hamilton, left the CSA and established a competing national association, the National Equal Franchise Union (NEFU). Previously the cause of the split has been attributed to 'personal ambition and pique.'[51] A closer examination of the break suggests that more than personality may have been at stake. The new association represented the social reform suffragists and took a more moderate stance on many controversial issues. The CSA on the other hand, or at least the CSA's executive, Dr Stowe-Gullen, Dr Gordon, and Mrs Denison, continued to outrage the public with their unreserved opinions and extremist views.

The programmes, priorities, and tactics of the CSA and the NEFU differed. The breakaway members, Constance Hamilton, Edith Lang, and Mrs G.I.H. Lloyd, were all newcomers to the suffrage movement, in contrast to the CSA executive who had carried the movement on their shoulders for the past fifteen years. The three recent converts came from the same social class as the original suffragists,[52] but while the CSA triumvirate all held jobs, the NEFU executive were housewives. As a result, in good Victorian tradition, the latter tended to look down upon women who condescended to work. They found the leadership of such women, especially of Mrs Denison who stooped so low as to rub shoulders with men in the business world, objectionable from every point of view.[53] As Honorary President, the NEFU selected a woman more to their taste, Lady Grace Julia Drummond.[54] Mrs Denison's son, Merrill Denison, pinpointed the social dichotomy between the groups when he explained that his mother was too much of a democrat for the likes of Mrs Hamilton and the other 'Rosedale socialites.'[55]

In an attempt to oust Mrs Denison and her associates, the NEFU branded them an 'anti-democratic oligarchy,' unwilling to make room for new officers, draw up a constitution, or arrange for annual meetings or regularly audited accounts.[56] The 'Old Guard,' it is true, invoked their seniority and refused to step aside for 'johnny-come-lately's' to the movement. After struggling through the hard times and occasionally financing the movement out of their own pockets, they felt that they deserved to reap some of the laurels. Perhaps, also, the women had seen the subsequent fate of early suffrage societies taken over by similar individuals, and were determined to retain control. Mrs Denison, at any rate, refused to surrender the decision-making to 'the new women of the Equal Franchise League, with only a few months' work to their credit': 'When a council of men and women have struggled with a proposition against all the inertia, prejudice, and ignorance of an age and at last have been instrumental in educating the public to the point where its reform is accepted so seriously that parliament is considering its claim – is it to be wondered at, if this council might think it their prerogative to decide the policy of a general meeting ...?'[57]

The NEFU accused the CSA, particularly Mrs Denison, of being tied up with the British militants, a position these respectable ladies refused to tolerate. It was no coincidence that both Mrs Lang and Mrs Lloyd, recent arrivals in Canada, held memberships in the constitutional British suffrage association, the National Union of Woman Suffrage Societies (NUWSS). In fact, the NEFU allied itself with the British constitutionalists and used the name 'the NUWSS of Canada' for the first year of its existence.[58]

Mrs Denison denied the charge of militancy, despite her sympathy for the Pankhursts and their tactics. Having worked for the suffrage for many more years than the ladies of the NEFU, however, Mrs Denison assumed a more aggressive attitude. She expressed her sincerest hope that militancy would be avoided in Canada but warned that the only way to do this was to enfranchise Canadian women.[59] Her threats never led to action, although she did manage to address one militant London demonstration in 1913, alienating the ultra-pacific majority in the Canadian movement.

The NEFU succeeded in attracting a large following from across the country, composed of dissidents who were tired of or discontented with the Toronto élite. The Beaches Progressive Club, the

Toronto Teachers' Suffrage Society, the Junior Suffrage Club all changed their allegiance to the NEFU. The Union's first executive included several well-known suffragists: Sara Rowell Wright of London (Ontario), sister of the Ontario Liberal and prohibition- ist leader Newton Rowell; Carrie Derick, President of the Mont- real Suffrage Association; and Mary Crawford, President of the Manitoba Political Equality League.[60] Nellie McClung, who had never been on good terms with Mrs Denison, also joined the new association.[61] Although it is impossible to estimate the actual numbers in the CSA and the NEFU, it would seem that the NEFU had become a major contender for suffrage support.

Based on the above sample, the NEFU clearly appealed to both working women and housewives. The movement did not split along these lines. The deciding factor seems to have been one's attitude towards the purpose of the reform. Those who joined the NEFU considered the opinions of the CSA too extreme. They wanted the vote as an expression of opinion but had no desire or intention to disrupt the traditional family structure.

The outbreak of war in 1914 divided the two bodies even more deeply and illustrated their different priorities. At the onset of hostilities, both the CSA and the NEFU endorsed the war effort, justified its necessity, and promised co-operation and support.[62] But when the NEFU suggested dropping the suffrage issue 'for the duration,' the CSA refused. Instead, it called for 'Business as Usual' and continued to send petitions and deputations throughout the war. In the opinion of its leaders, the suffrage issue superseded even national emergency.[63] The NEFU on the contrary supported a multiplicity of reform causes and was less committed to a suffrage victory. It also seemed more susceptible to patriotic, nativistic appeals, a weakness the politicans later exploited in the Wartime Elections Act. Its President, Constance Hamilton, con- demned the CSA for spending money, time, and energy on a cam- paign which divided women at a point when 'the united efforts of the women of Canada should be put in valiant service for the empire.'[64] The CSA executive, meanwhile, refused to become un- questioning patriots and kept an open mind on the whole issue of war and peace. In 1916 it sponsored a lecture by the well- known pacifist, Newton Wylie, on 'Woman Suffrage and Universal Peace.' The NEFU was outraged. It denied any connection with the lecture and declared that it had 'no intention of discussing any aspect of peace until the war is over.'[65]

The organizational split at the national level confirms the deeper ideological division within the movement. Canada, it seems, had parallel suffrage movements. A small feminist clique set up the organizational appartus to conduct the campaign, but it was overwhelmed numerically and ideologically by male and female social reformers who had more moderate goals for the movement. Through their domination, the movement in Canada lost its association with feminist causes.

3

The Political Ideas of the Suffragists

Many Canadian suffragists themselves recognized two approaches to the suffrage question, the feminist and the social reform approach. Flora Macdonald Denison distinguished between 'social service suffragists,' those with a prior commitment to reform, and 'real suffragists,' those who believed that 'men and women should be born equally free and independent members of the human race ...'[1] The categories, quite clearly, were not exclusive. Most feminists were also enthusiastic, dedicated social reformers. Even Mrs Denison, a leading feminist, felt sure that woman suffrage would rectify crimes against childhood and other social evils. Otherwise, she emphasized, she would not work for it another day.[2] The distinction was one of degree, not kind.

Similar distinctions characterized the suffragists' political ideology. Since all believed in some or other social reform, all accepted a degree of state intervention. But, within this broad area of agreement, there existed many variations which represented the diverse shades of political opinion of the day, ranging from a point just left of orthodox laissez faire to a point a little right of socialism. This range of attitudes suggests that a similar spectrum existed within the larger reform movement.

I

The suffragists' political ideology was a product of the changed circumstances of industrial life. Urban life had eroded the old faith in cutthroat competition, independence, and self-help. In the city, slums and diseases threatened the whole population. The health of one became the health of all. In the words of the Montreal Recorder and suffragist, Robert Stanley Weir, 'The body politic is like the human body in that the infection of any one part causes the whole to suffer.'[3] Poverty and unemployment could no longer be safely ignored, according to an 1889 Quebec WCTU Report: 'Our paths may not lead down to the city slums or within the prison walls, but this "monster of so frightful mein" comes up to our hearthstones.'[4] Although young, Canada had begun to bear an ominous resemblance to the Old World with its slums, its poverty, and its discontents.[5]

Large aggregations of capital, 'the interests,' 'the trusts,' 'Big Business,' – reform rhetoric borrowed from the United States almost before the situation existed in Canada – towered above the little man, challenging his liberty and his control over his own life. As capitalism depended upon the free interplay of equal units, Big Business, particularly cartels and monopolies, upset the balance and made free enterprise a fondly remembered myth.

Political philosophy responded to these changes in the economy. Few historians would continue to defend Dicey's strict distinction between individualism and collectivism;[6] however, political ideology in the nineteenth century definitely evolved in the direction of greater government intervention. Party lines blurred over the issue. According to one study of British Victorian politics by George Watson, no political party in Britain believed in or practised complete laissez faire and no philosopher defended it. The Liberals, Watson suggests, always accepted a role for government in the national economy. 'They debated not whether it should exist, but what it should be.'[7] A second study, which traces developments within the British Conservative Party in this period, maintains that the traditional conservative defence of state authority made it easier for Conservatives 'to adopt a cautiously pragmatic approach to social reforms' than for their Liberal rivals who were closely identified with classical British economics.[8]

Jeremy Bentham, the man usually credited with enunciating orthodox laissez faire liberalism, wished to reduce government interference in the economy in order to sweep away those things that stood in the way of the English industrialist. His attack was directed against feudal law, primogeniture, the tariff, apprenticeship, old poor laws, sinecures and extravagant government, and nepotism in Church and State.[9] Hence he became associated with the dictum that the state which governs least, governs best. On an individual level, he defined liberty to mean that each man ought to be free to pursue his own interests. But even Bentham admitted a role for the government. He defended the retention of a gently paternal state which would not interfere directly with individuals, except criminals, but which would encourage correct behaviour with suitable rewards and punishments. Prizes, for example, were to be offered for inventions! Manchesterian economics, however, had difficulty explaining away the findings of Charles Booth or Seebohm Rowntree or answering the social criticism of Thomas Carlyle, John Ruskin, William Morris, George Bernard Shaw, Sidney Webb, Arnold Toynbee, and H.G. Wells.[10] In an industrial society, Bentham's individual liberty became an illusion for all but a powerful and affluent minority who made life uncomfortable for the rest of society.

John Stuart Mill attempted to humanize utilitarianism by adding to it the principle of self-protection, which, in Mill's words, is 'the sole end for which mankind are warranted, individually or collectively, in interfering with the liberty or action of any of their number.'[11] This proviso admitted the intervention of the government, the only tool available to the common man to protect the larger, general interest against unscrupulous individuals, but its function was still largely negative. According to Mill, 'The only purpose for which power can be rightfully exercised over any member of a civilized community, against his will, is to prevent harm to others. His own good, either physical or moral, is not a sufficient warrant.'[12]

T.H. Green's political theory is often described as the principal link connecting the Old Liberalism of the Manchester School to the New Liberalism which inspired the social legislation enacted by the Asquith government before 1914. Crane Brinton argues that Green's idealist metaphysics provided the necessary basis for the transition from laissez faire to state regulation.[13] Green redefined liberty to mean not simply the freedom *from* legal restraint but a more positive freedom, the freedom *to* do good. In his opinion, since the state represented the 'accumulated efforts of generations' of men striving to translate their aspirations into reality, it offered a higher rationality than is found in the individual and, therefore, the good man would do well to conform to its dictates. In other words, the state could define what the good life entailed.

Green was still far from collectivism in the strict sense. He consistently maintained a presumption against state action when other means existed.[14] He distinguished between moral and political freedom and argued that a strictly moral act is done voluntarily, as an end in itself, without regard for any enforcing agent. He continued to defend the idea of self-help and felt that the state should only do for people what they are unable to do for themselves. The ultimate aim of Green's state was to create a social environment in which moral men could operate, and he justified using state interference to remove obstructions to moral behaviour. On these grounds he defended compulsory education, for 'Without a command of certain elementary arts and knowledge, the individual in modern society is as effectually crippled as by the loss of a limb.' The state also had a responsibility to remove such anomalies as religious discrimination and class-based land laws. Finally, Green endorsed prohibition on the grounds that the state 'ought to aid those who could not aid themselves to become temperate.'[15]

While the Conservatives did not provide the theorists to justify their shift in direction, both Arthur Balfour and Lord Salisbury displayed a 'hesitant benevolence' towards the working classes. Two other prominent Conservative politicans, Randolph Churchill and Joseph Chamberlain, presented a more constructive approach to social problems. Churchill advocated a new 'Tory democracy' based upon the realization that the masses were naturally conservative and that, therefore, a Conservative Party should adopt a policy to satisfy them. Chamberlain recognized that 'a movement for social legislation is in the air' and argued that the Conservatives should guide it. His programme included payment of MPs, an eight-hour day for miners, the establishment of arbitration tribunals for trade disputes, labour exchanges, workmen's compensation, and old age pensions.[16]

Canada's suffragists in general accepted the trend towards increased state intervention. All had moved beyond orthodox laissez faire liberalism. The slogans they used to describe their philosophy were products of the prevalent idealism of the day and indicate a consensus regarding the need for collective action in the modern industrialized world. James Hughes, for example, referred to an 'unselfish, progressive aim to make the world better,' Flora Macdonald Denison appealed to the 'social soul,' and Mrs John Cox, a Montreal suffragist, to the 'corporate conscience,' a 'sense of our interdependence.'[17] They redefined liberty to allow room for state intervention. Mrs Denison, for example, maintained that 'your Personal Liberty stops just where society's begins,' a précis of Mill's classic definition.[18] Another Toronto suffragist, Margaret Carlyle, a factory inspector, to whom the question of government intervention was a real and vital issue, defended 'the great principle of the greatest good of the greatest number, even if it does demand some small personal sacrifice.'[19]

They were, of course, not socialists. The majority were liberal reformers of the Mill and Green variety who called for equality of opportunity, not equality of condition. They believed that captalism could work and would work but only if each citizen was guaranteed an equal start, an open road for advancement, and some protection against the contingencies of life. The state had only to provide an 'even chance' for everyone by removing all artificial restrictions which barred the way to 'progress, development, and advancement.'[20] A smaller number were committed Conservatives, notably Sarah Curzon and James L. Hughes in Toronto, Mrs John Scott in Montreal, Ella Hatheway in New Brunswick, and Helen Gregory MacGill in British Columbia. Woman suffrage was not strictly a party issue. The Conservative suffragists represented a strain of Canadian 'Tory democracy' and unanimously endorsed the growth of state authority and responsibility.

Within this broad consensus, however, the suffragists disagreed on the amount and kind of state intervention needed. Some had advanced as far as the early Mill,[21] who advocated the use of the state as policeman, to prevent one person from abusing another's liberty. Factory and minimum wage laws are an example of this type of legislation. Many turned to the state for protection against the 'interests,' again primarily a negative, defensive function. Another group advanced a more positive view of the function of good government. One Manitoba suffragist, paraphrasing Green, asked that the state safeguard the interests of the governed 'not only in the matter of the prevention of harm but in the cultivation of that which makes for good.'[22] Temperance advocates took this to mean that you could force men to be free, thereby justifying prohibition.[23]

Almost invariably, those outspoken on feminist issues stood farthest to the left politically. Emily Stowe fell under the influence of her sister, Hannah A. Kimball of Chicago, a devotee of the American reformer Edward Bellamy. Speaking under the auspices of the Canadian Commonwealth Federation and the Anti-Poverty Association, she publicly endorsed Henry George's idea of the single tax on land values, labour exchanges, and something she called 'Fraternal Socialism.'[24] Flora Macdonald Denison also had a reputation as an ardent critic of capitalism. In 1898 she declared that 'With the competitive system in full blast and the premiums on the successful competitor, falsehood is catered to, the sweating system becomes a necessity and hundreds go under that a few may be on top ...'[25] Her city of the future would be a 'great hospital home,' guaranteeing employment and comfort to all within its gates.[26] Margaret Blair Gordon belonged to both the Single Tax Association and the Public Ownership League which advocated nationalization of public utilities.

The majority, in contrast, had a very limited vision of what the interests of the governed entailed. Generally they advocated using the government to remove only the most glaring evils and inequalities of the system. To Ethel Hurlbatt of the Montreal Suffrage Association, the key problems were inadequate accommodation, tenement buildings, and lack of fresh air.[27] While not consciously self-seeking, they concentrated on the areas of reform which, if left untended, threatened their own health, security, and way of life. The Montreal suffragist Robert Stanley

Weir, for example, asked only for the provision of better housing for the poor, for freer and purer forms of public amusement, prevention of the spread of contagion by more ample hospital facilities, a strict enforcement of the license laws relating to the retail sale of intoxicating beverages, and constant efforts to keep up the 'moral tone' of the community.[28]

The suffragists' attitudes towards the problem of poverty illustrate the shades of difference within their political philosophy. All unanimously condemned private, individual charity because of its inability to cope with the magnitude of the problem. Corporate charity, still voluntary but organized and anonymous, found many more adherents as it promised greater efficiency and a wider field of coverage. The Charity Organization Society (COS), an idea which originated in Britain in 1869 and which reached Canada in 1901, proved particularly popular. It attracted only the more reluctant interventionists, however, since it contained an old laissez faire assumption that the poor are so through choice. The COS deliberately made the reception of charity as unpleasant as possible in order to discourage paupers from remaining on the dole.[29] The question of the recipient's character seemed more at issue than his suffering.

A few more socially aware suffragists demanded government-managed relief as a matter of justice, not pity. Recognizing that many, through no fault of their own, became ill or unemployed, Francis Marion Beynon recommended a system of state-managed relief run in conjunction with a comprehensive chain of employment bureaus.[30] The Kingston author and suffragist Agnes Maule Machar asked that the state assume complete responsibility for orphans, mental and physical cripples, and the aged.[31]

Idealism, as a theory of state interference, was profoundly ambiguous. Considered purely logically, Green's emphasis on individual character gave as much support to the COS as his theory of positive government gave to the New Liberals.[32] Perhaps this confusion is due to the attempt by liberals to advance a new social ideology while retaining their intense faith in the individual. In a recent interpretation of John Stuart Mill, Gertrude Himmelfarb argues that this dichotomy exists throughout Mill's writings. On the one hand he defends 'absolute' liberty and the 'sovereign' individual, yet on the other he endorses a variety of social and historical forces to counteract the tyranny of the masses.[33] The suffragists frequently invoked the theme of 'woman's individuality' and 'individual worth' to justify their claim to the ballot. Like Mill, they had just as much difficulty reconciling this view with their willingness to restrict the liberty of other classes in order to ensure peace and harmony.

II

Even given the wide range within the suffragists' political attitudes, it is still possible to distinguish ideologically between a suffragist and an anti-suffragist. Since Canada had a weak suffrage movement, it evoked little strong opposition. A group of Toronto women, led by Mrs H.D. Warren, the wife of a Toronto businessman, organized Canada's only Anti-Suffrage Society. A few Canadian intellectuals contributed to the debate, however, making it possible to assess their political philosophy.

Anti-suffragists typically expressed a distrust of democracy. They upheld an organic conception of society and feared that democracy undermined the organism by dividing it into competing individuals. Andrew Macphail, a well-known Canadian intellectual and anti-suffragist, compared democracy to a cancer which 'strives to destroy the organs and organization of society, which strives to reduce races, nations, and families to unorganized congeries of individuals.'[34] Democracy to his mind was not a species of government; it was the chaos out of which government developed. The Toronto suffragist Sonia Leathes went to the heart of their argument when she observed that 'Some people say they do not believe in woman suffrage but what they really do not believe in is representative government.'[35]

The organic view of society rested upon the family. Consequently woman suffrage held a special fear for the anti-suffragist. Not only would it compound the evil of individualistic democracy but it threatened to divide the family into separate individuals as well. They felt that as a unit the family required only one representative, the husband. An outspoken suffrage opponent, the retired Manchester Liberal Goldwin Smith, argued that female enfranchisement would set husband against wife, brother against sister, destroying the harmony of the home and undermining the strength of community and family ties.[36]

The family constituted an important element in the suffragists' scheme of things as well, but they interpreted the effects of woman suffrage very differently. They maintained that by giving the separate individuals in the family separate votes you doubled the political representation of the family and consequently doubled its strength. The ends were basically the same – to bolster the status quo. Only the means differed. By trusting in 'purified' democracy, the suffragists offered a more sophisticated solution to society's ills.

The anti-suffragists felt that they had valid evidence to support their case against the 'new woman.' They attributed both a decreasing birth rate and an increasing divorce rate to woman's new independence and maintained that giving her a vote would encourage these trends. A vocal Toronto anti-suffragist, Clementia Fessenden, feared that women were already increasingly avoiding the responsibilities of 'Motherhood' and 'If those [responsibilities] of nation-management were added, it was hard to say where the end would be.'[37] The suffragists argued exactly the reverse. They maintained that women could easily be both mothers and voters. The whole purpose of enfranchising women, they maintained, was to extend the maternal influence into society, not to see it destroyed.

Both suffragists and anti-suffragists feared that extra-familial occupations for women might undermine homelife. Stephen Leacock became an anti-suffragist because he believed that the right to vote would encourage female independence and discourage marriage. He raised the cry of race suicide: 'It is quite impossible for women – the average and ordinary women – to go in for having a career. Nature has forbidden it. The average woman must necessarily have ... about three and one quarter children. If she fails to do this the population comes to an end.'[38] Most suffragists would have accepted this analysis. But they could not understand why Leacock anticipated that female enfranchisement would create career-minded women. *They* wanted votes in order to be effective mothers.

Consistent with their suspicion of democracy, the anti-suffragists had little confidence in the power of legislation. Consequently, they disapproved of the women's intense desire to share in the making of laws. The McGill professor Warwick Chipman criticized the tendency to 'propose laws on every subject and to constantly exhort state interference.' To his mind women voters would simply multiply the mass of laws. A mother's duty, according to Chipman, was to keep the home fire burning and to tend to the spiritual and physical needs of her children for 'It is these that keep the world pure and good, rather than the *cold forms of the law.*'[39]

A basic confusion characterized the anti-suffrage ideology, paralleling that in the suffrage mind. The suffragists defended individualism but were willing to compromise it to achieve certain social goals. The anti-suffragists considered individualism destructive but felt equally uncomfortable with its alternative, state interference. Both groups were essentially socially conservative. They differed only in that the anti-suffragists wished to preserve the old order sacrosanct and immutable while the suffragists were willing to accept minor modifications to guarantee the perpetuation of that order.

III

While it seems fair to call the anti-suffragists 'anti-democratic,' this by no means makes the suffragists supreme democrats. Like most Victorian liberals, the suffragists greeted democracy with a 'welcome tinged with warning.'[40] Walter Bagehot feared handing over government to 'the jangled mass of men.' Even Mill argued that liberty could be trusted to the masses only in certain circumstances. Implicit in the philosophy of both Mill and Green is the need for a ruling élite, based less on inherited rights and prerogatives than on acquired talent. If the function of the state, as Green maintained, was to provide the 'good life' for its citizens, we must ask who is to determine what the 'good life' entails.

Education played the chief role in the creation of this meritorious hierarchy. It developed the mind, the rational in man, but it did more than this. Victorian idealism was in part a reaction against the purely rational. Education possessed an added primary virtue of character formation – it made men good. Consequently, every suffragist, with the exception of a few radical democrats like the Manitoba suffragist Francis Marion Beynon, defended the need for an intelligence or educational qualification for the vote.[41] Even the TWLS accepted this limitation to democracy. In fact, at first the TWLS had endorsed the basic principle of British conservatism, that only property ought to be represented. But by 1880 the Society ruled that many intelligent votes were being lost through the defects of the property qualification and that the true basis of the franchise ought therefore to rest in knowledge.[42]

An educational qualification for voting suited the women's purposes well. Generally well-educated themselves, they could argue that this entitled them to membership in the ruling élite. Education also served as a sex solvent since it obliterated the distinctions between men and women and raised them to a measurable standard of equality. In a society in which strength and force still wielded power, it made sense for the women to look for equality in their mental capacity.

But the suffragists' faith in education was more than pragmatic; they genuinely believed that it gave them an insight into the needs of the community. They considered themselves 'the thinkers among the masses,' 'men and women whose ideals are lofty' and 'who have control of our appetites and passions.'[43] Consequently, they did not hesitate to impose their ideals upon the whole population. Paternalistic moralism justified prohibition, for example. Nellie McClung argued that if liquor 'isn't safe for everyone, it isn't safe for anyone.'[44]

The suffragists felt that they had a duty to boost the less fortunate, to make the ignorant aware of the 'good life.' Consequently, they appear little more enamoured of popular government than the anti-suffragists. Their democracy had very definite limits. The individual achieved a new importance in their system, but the type of individual who would be allowed to exert influence would be very closely regulated. Foreigners, for example, were clearly suspect. Unaccustomed to political demo-

First Free Enlightened Elector – 'Whatta you tinka dis votes for
women?' Second Free Enlightened Elector – 'Tommyrot! Why,
they've got to be eddicated up to it fust.'
Montreal Herald, Woman's Edition, 26 November 1913

cracy, they became the target of dishonest political interests. The Alberta suffragist Emily Murphy told an anecdote about an Italian immigrant who sent home the message: 'Come to Canada, all of you, they give you a vote out here and then give you $2 for it.'[45] Her meaning was clear.

The immigrant's political malleability was not his only vice, however. As members of a Protestant, Anglo-Saxon élite, the suffragists had a vision of a homogeneous, Christian Canada which the presence of large unassimilable immigrant groups challenged. The example of the United States, where foreigners had flooded into the country unchecked, frightened them. Rev R.W. Dickie, a Presbyterian clergyman and a member of the Montreal Suffrage Association, cautioned his audience that 'We are receiving more [immigrants] according to our population than the United States ever received and it is our duty to see that Christian principles and Christian institutions be planted in their life.'[46]

Many reforms in the suffragist programme aimed specifically at cleansing, Christianizing, and assimilating the immigrant. Through prohibition, the suffragists hoped to impose sober Protestant standards on wine-making foreigners. The demand for legislation to raise the age of consent for girls arose, in part, in response to testimony at the 1905 Dominion WCTU Convention that brides were being sold into slavery among 'the debased population of southern Europe.'[47] The suffragists endorsed compulsory education primarily because they believed it to be the only truly effective means of transforming the immigrant into a Canadian. In the West, the majority favoured an 'English only' policy in the first six years of public schooling, to remove 'the large colonies of people in our provinces who have not adequate knowledge of the English language.'[48]

Isobel Graham, a contributor to the *Grain Growers' Guide* and a member of the Manitoba Political Equality League, conducted an overtly racist campaign for equal homesteading rights for British-born and Canadian women. As she explained in a letter to Mrs F.H. Torrington, President of the NCW in 1913, the whole purpose of the crusade was to help equalize the balance in the Prairies on behalf of the native population. She asked: 'Are we

Western farmers so cultured, so steadfast, so loyal, so philanthropic that we can bear dilution by the ignorance, low idealism, and religious perversity of the average foreigner?' She implored her audience to 'Keep back the foreigner. Give us good, sound British stock – women already British, already civilized, already subjected to both earth and heaven for conduct.'[49]

Generally Canadians remained confident of their ability to assimilate most immigrants, save perhaps those of a different colour, the blacks and the Orientals. Black immigration in the period was slight. Yet the same Mrs Graham lamented the 'negro invasion.' She deplored the atrocities and outrages against white women committed by members of these 'terrible communities,' and recommended, as punishment, lynching or burning at the stake.[50] Alison Craig, another Manitoba suffragist, had an equally unfriendly welcome for the Hindu or East Indian who, she claimed, by 'sheer force of numbers' would submerge the hemisphere.[51]

A few women had a more open-minded attitude. Emily Murphy admired certain immigrant traits: for example, the Ukrainian's peasant values and the Doukhobor's deep religiosity. She still wished to see them Canadianized but recommended more subtle methods. Canadians teaching them citizenship, language, and laws ought in her opinion to adopt a 'sympathetic respect for their pride and a wise patience.'[52] Mrs Murphy also had her racist side, however. In *Black Candle*, her study of the opium trade in the West, she included sensationalist photos of black men lounging alongside opium-intoxicated white women. Perhaps, she warned, the Chinese and Negro dope pedlars were unconscious emissaries of superiors intent on the downfall of the white race. She further supported the total exclusion from Canada of the 'prolific Germans,' 'the equally prolific Russians,' and 'the still more fertile yellow races' who threatened to wrest the leadership of the world from the British.[53]

The foreigner provided powerful rhetoric to advance the cause of female enfranchisement. Believing that the right to vote ought to depend upon one's ability to vote, particularly upon one's intelligence, the women found it frustrating to be disfranchised while untutored Ruthenians and Galicians determined their

'Everybody Votes but Mother.' *Grain Growers' Guide*, 1 July 1914

laws. The female franchise, they argued, without apology, was needed to offset the increased numbers of illiterate immigrants and paupers. The Saskatchewan PEFB demonstrated statistically how the enfranchisement of women could right the balance in favour of the native-born: 'Male immigrants to this country out-number the female 2 to 1. The enfranchisement of women would increase the proportion of native-born electors. It is proportions, not numbers that determine elections.'[54] Capitalizing on the belief in woman's moral superiority, they insisted that good Christian women could perform equally as well as, if not better than, the foreigner. They also invoked their nativity and their patriotism. Margaret McAlpine of the CSA, for example, explained to Sir Wilfrid Laurier in 1911 that 'Canadian women have the well-being of the country more at heart than the average foreign immigrant.'[55]

This rationale transformed many male reformers into suffragists. The prohibitionist and well-known *Grip* cartoonist, J.W. Bengough, also a devoted member of the DWEA, saw in female enfranchisement 'the off-setting of an electoral element largely evil by the introduction of an element largely good.' It would, he explained, increase the native vote against the foreign, the educated against the ignorant, the moral against the vicious.[56] James Hughes, similarly, could not understand why ignorant foreigners, uneducated men of native birth, and weak young men without experience or training were allowed to vote while the most cultured and intelligent women were refused this right simply becuase they were women.[57] Nativism played a significant role both in winning converts to the suffrage cause and in its eventual success.

IV

Like democracy, industrialization both enchanted and alarmed the suffragists. The pace of city life with its total disregard for the Protestant virtues of family, morality, piety, and sobriety distressed them. Ideally they longed to return to the land. The agrarian myth of 'peace and security and plenty'[58] strongly appealed to them. The grasping materialism of industrialization offended their sensibility and threatened their design for a meritocracy of intellectuals. Annie B. Jamieson, a British Columbia educator and suffragist, fought against 'the encroachments of a materialism everywhere present and threatening to engulf us.' She hoped the university would become for women 'the ideal in the midst of the material' and an avenue to future seats of power.[59]

While loathing the materialism and social devastation, however, the suffragists became intrigued with the industrial mechanism. It created a methodical regimentation of life which fascinated them. It stood for the ruthless elimination of waste and inefficiency. It required a society in its place and on time. The suffragists and their fellow reformers were equally disturbed by the restlessness and confusion they observed in the world around them. They decided to transform society into a well-run corporation by applying the iron rules of industrial production to the social order. 'Efficiency,' 'control,' 'planning' became the key words in their programme. Several studies confirm this reform preoccupation with 'technical rationality.'[60]

The problem of political corruption caused them particular distress. Revelations of purchased votes, closely allied to the 'demon rum,' graft in public works, rake-offs in purchasing departments, and the bribing of aldermen by the representatives of 'great corporations with favours to ask' naturally alarmed reformers who hoped to use the state as an instrument of reform.[61] They blamed party politics for much of the evil. The Saskatchewan Franchise Board on one occasion debated the proposition that 'the system of party government is detrimental to the welfare of democracy.'[62] Two remedies, 'direct legislation' and the creation of boards of experts, despite the obvious ideological contradictions between them, both found supporters in the movement.

The more democratic of the two, direct legislation, comprised a trio of reforms designed to win the legislatures back into the control of the people. The 'initiative' allowed a portion of the population to initiate legislation; the 'referendum' permitted the people to voice an opinion on a specific piece of legislation; the 'recall' enabled the people to remove from office any politician who failed to live up to his promises. The Saskatchewan PEFB and the Ontario Woman Citizens' Association, the successor to the Ontario Woman Franchise Association, both included in their platforms requests that candidates to the legislature be subject to recall.[63] The Saskatchewan Board added that candidates should be free representatives, free that is from political machines, that amounts subscribed to party funds be publicized, that patronage be abolished, and that civil service examinations be made competitive. Several male suffragists belonged to the Direct Legislation League, started in 1906.[64]

The desire for efficiency, on the other hand, made many suffragists support the idea of appointed Boards of Control, composed of experts in their fields, to replace elected, ward politicians. Since municipal government dealt with the day-to-day health and convenience of the people, reformers saw the benefits of a prompt, businesslike service, a civic corporation, so to speak. Appointment rather than election would, they hoped, place these officials above the temptations of bribery.[65] But since the expert élite stood outside and above the control of the electorate, the price was a less democratic government. In both Montreal and Toronto, suffragists participated in the local campaigns for Boards of Control.

Facing the choice between efficiency and democracy, the suffragists often preferred the former. The dichotomy in their attitude towards industrialization, their abhorrence of its grubby materialism and their infatuation with its precision, left them open to the seduction of bureaucrats and social experts. 'Rule by expert' seemed to promise the application to society of the lessons of industry while it relieved the intellectuals of the distasteful task of worrying about such mundane matters. Milton Rokeach describes the Canadian reformers when he writes that, although their programme appeared humanistic in content, the structure designed to implement it became impersonal and bureaucratic because of the desire for businesslike administration.[66] The confusion between ends and means produced inner inconsistencies and eventual disillusionment in the mind of many a reformer and contributed to the eclipse of reform in the years following World War I.

The suffragists were optimists and idealists who hoped to create a new, better-ordered society in Canada. They had a very precise vision of what that society would look like and were not hesitant, in the slightest, to impose their blueprint upon the whole population. Government intervention, in fact, provided the means to do just that. Through state planning and control, they hoped to establish an efficient, orderly structure in which they and their allies, the natural ruling élite, would be the directors. Predictably the women in the movement wanted the means, a political voice, to impose their desires upon the legislature.

While these women were carving out positions of power and respect for themselves, they subscribed to an ideology which restricted the role options available to other women in the community. The reform movement which they joined wished only to moderate the pace of change and had no desire to modify seriously institutions like the family. A breakdown and analysis of this movement in its several segments will demonstrate that the ideology of reform made a feminist analysis of women's problems both inappropriate and unpopular.

4

In Defence of the Church

Several historians have noted the close connection between the Protestant Churches and the social reform movement of the late nineteenth and early twentieth centuries.[1] The revelation of declining Church memberships and poor attendance at services convinced some Protestants, and a few Catholics, to make their message more socially relevant. This led to the enunciation of a social gospel which stated that Christians had a duty to remove visible social ills and help to create Christ's Kingdom on earth. Their good works would testify to their salvation.

The social gospel played an important role in the political awakening of women. Clearly, good, Christian women had a responsibility to respond to the injunction to do the Lord's work. As a result many joined evangelical associations; many became missionaries; many became more actively committed to reform. These extra-familial duties made women aware of current social problems and the political disability they faced by not having a vote. As a result, some joined suffrage societies.

At the same time, however, the Church upheld the traditional social structure based upon the home and the woman in the home. In its view, the vast majority of women were predestined, pre-ordained housewives and mothers. The new areas of Church work were meant to be restricted to widows or spinsters or to mothers with grown-up children. Women were excluded from the ordained ministry; they were still considered primarily helpmates.[2] On balance, therefore, while the social gospel encouraged a degree of political activism, it constrained women by keeping them tied to traditional roles. As we shall see, the radical feminists who challenged sex stereotyping usually moved outside the traditional Churches.

I

The rise of the city presented traditional religion with its most severe challenge. There was a distinct falling off in church attendance in the cities. Clergy were proving difficult to recruit and even that 'most stubborn of Victorian institutions, the Sabbath, was beginning to yield to new pressures.'[3] Industry tried to override the Puritan Sunday for profit's sake. The indifference and fatigue of the working classes took an even greater toll.

Decreasing memberships aggravated apprehensions about lost prestige and authority in some denominations more than others. Canada's Methodist Church, closely associated with English-Canadian nationalist aspirations, suffered a marked decline from 17 per cent of Canada's population in 1881 to 14.98 per cent in 1911. Baptists in the same period dropped from 6.86 per cent to 5.31 per cent. The Presbyterians remained stable at 15.68 per cent while the Anglicans suffered a temporary decline from 13.35 per cent in 1881 to 12.69 per cent in 1901 but recouped their losses during the next decade to register 14.47 per cent in 1911.[4]

Meanwhile the small pockets of foreigners who professed a different religious faith continued to grow. The Lutherans advanced from 1.06 per cent to 3.19 per cent between 1881 and 1911 and the Greek Church, nonexistent in 1881, registered 1.23 per cent in 1911. More unorthodox groups made inroads also. The Eastern religions, Hindus, Buddhists, and Sikhs, represented 0.39 per cent in 1911 and Mormons, 0.22 per cent. While the percentages might seem insignificant, the numbers, approximately twenty-nine thousand and sixteen thousand respectively, and the alien character of the creeds presented a direct challenge to traditional Christianity.

This explains the dominant nativist strain in works like J.S. Woodsworth's *My Neighbour* and *Strangers Within Our Gates* or

C.W. Gordon's *The Foreigner*. The obvious solution to the problem lay in conversion. The introduction to *Strangers Within Our Gates* proclaimed; '*There is a danger and it is national!* Either we must educate and elevate the incoming multitudes or they will drag us and our children down to a lower level.'[5] Christianizing and Canadianizing were considered two parts of the same process since 'Protestant ideals and values were seen as an integral part of Anglo-Saxon civilization.'[6]

Many Christians began to suspect that the Church was stagnating because its message had lost social relevance for large numbers of people. The writings of British and American social critics and social scientists, such as Carlyle, Tennyson, Thoreau, Benjamin Kidd, Arnold Toynbee, Edward Bellamy, and Henry George, drew attention to the pressing social distress of the urban populace. Woodsworth recognized the problem: 'The Church, as an organization, does not exercise the predominating influence in the lives of its members that once it did ... it is not to-day coping successfully with the great social problems which in their acutest form, are found in the city ... Perhaps its programme is too limited.'[7]

In response the Churches dropped their obsession with theological dogma and began emphasizing the physical and social needs of their parishioners. All the Protestant denominations, and even the Roman Catholics,[8] shared, though in different degrees, in the new social awakening. Methodism had a long tradition of social awareness, going back to John Wesley, who insisted that his was a 'social religion.'[9] In the decades between 1880 and 1910 the Canadian Methodist Church became a principal vehicle of the social gospel. Whereas in 1880 the Canadian Methodists seemed committed to a doctrinal religious mission, by 1910 their aim was 'nothing less than the establishment of Christ's Kingdom on earth.'[10] In the Presbyterian and Anglican Churches a tradition of strong paternalism found expression in the social service movement. Moreover, Canadian Presbyterianism had been stimulated by the evangelical influences of the Free Kirk movement.[11]

Richard Allen has suggested that there were three categories of social gospeller, according to their political philosophy. To the right stood those who gave precedence to prohibition and other legislation designed to restrain individual impulse. The centre party favoured a broader welfare programme, including factory laws, a minimum wage, and maximum hours. Those on the left forecast a vast overhaul of the existing order.[12] Joy Parr has identified a similar dichotomy between *two* branches in the new evangelicalism. Ignoring the radicals, she differentiates between those who simply expanded their commitment to save the individual and those who decided that the *environment* produced sin and set out to change it.[13] This distinction closely resembles Paul Boyer's dual model of progressive thought: one wave dedicated to imposing their morals on society, the other favouring a legislative reordering of society.[14]

From the previous chapter, it is clear that members of the suffrage societies fell into both camps. Some were preoccupied with a campaign to improve society's morals and were generally content to use the state to restrict liberties. The prohibitionists were in this category. Moving to the left, a significant number advocated a much wider use of government intervention, and were convinced that improvements in the environment would produce a healthier society. Because of this broader awareness of social conditions, this latter group have been labelled 'secular' in this study, though religion may still have been an inspiration to many.[15]

II

The new evangelical crusade required an army of workers, teachers, and helpmates. Women, the majority[16] and reputedly the most pious members of the congregation, provided a vast, untapped reservoir of strong, devoted 'crusaders for Christ.' The Church conscripted them to service in Home and Foreign Missions, Deaconess Societies, Epworth Leagues, and Christian Endeavour Organizations.

The Methodist Women's Missionary Society, founded in 1881, had workers on two fronts, in the Far East and in the Canadian West where they established reformatories for wayward girls and worked in the foreign settlements. In the period after 1904 the Methodist WMS opened a Ruthenian House for Girls in Edmonton, a Settlement House in Regina, All People's Mission in Winnipeg, the Turner Institute at Vancouver, and Missions in Sydney, Ottawa, Hamilton, Welland, Toronto, and Windsor. In 1900 over fifteen thousand women belonged to the Methodist Society; that same year the corresponding Presbyterian WMS had twenty-six thousand members.[17]

The deaconess was the Protestant answer to the Catholic nun. Methodist and Presbyterian Deaconess Training Homes, established in Canada towards the end of the nineteenth century, produced teachers and nurses to work among the alien immigrants or aid the poor and the sick. Some moved into the wider fields of city missions and organized charity.[18] The opening of these new avenues to social work had a beneficial side-effect, making it permissible, even admirable, for women to participate actively in reforming endeavours.

The Methodist Conference and the Presbyterian and Anglican synods soon took the next logical step. Convinced that good, Christian women could act as a counterweight to the immigrant and the pauper, all three passed resolutions endorsing woman suffrage. Several Protestant ministers, usually those most committed to the social gospel, actually joined suffrage societies. For example, Rev Herbert Symonds, an Anglican, and Rev George Adam, a Congregationalist, were both members of the Montreal Suffrage Association; Rev Dr James Logan Gordon, Honorary President of the Manitoba Political Equality League, Rev Daniel S. Hamilton, second Vice-President of the Manitoba League, and Rev Dr Hugh Pedley, Honorary Vice-President of the Montreal Association in 1914, were all well-known for their advanced social views.[19]

At the Social Service Congress in Canada, held in Ottawa in 1914, the bond between woman suffrage and the social gospel was clear. The Congress, called by historian Richard Allen the 'culmination of social gospel ideology,' passed a resolution in favour of women's enfranchisement, welcomed delegates from the local suffrage society, and listened to addresses by two active suffragists, Sara Rowell Wright of London, Ontario and Rose Henderson of Montreal. The speakers, Dr Charles J.O. Hastings,

Toronto's medical health officer, and Rev W.M. Andrews, Methodist President of Saskatchewan College, both had wives who were suffragists. Four others, the prominent Labour leader and Toronto civic politician James Simpson, Toronto Controller J.O. McCarthy, the child welfare reformer J.J. Kelso, and Rev C.W. Gordon, better known to Canadian readers as Ralph Connor, all verbally supported woman suffrage on this and other occasions.[20]

On the other side, the social gospel awakened Christian women to their social duty. Women were instructed that, like the men, they had an obligation to earn their salvation through good works. They were told that they, as individuals, had an 'individual responsibility' to spread the faith and reform the world.[21] Protestant clerics condemned the traditional middle-class woman's laziness and lack of productivity. The Rev B.F. Austin, principal of Alma College in Belleville, told his female students that 'Labour of some kind is the great law of God written on woman's nature as it is on man's and to both sexes alike it is the highway to health, happiness, and success.'[22]

Undoubtedly sermons of this kind had a profound effect on the women in the audience. Several suffragists attributed their social awakening directly to religious injunction. Elizabeth Smith-Shortt, for example, thanked the Protestant ministers for stirring women out of their apathy, for making them long to 'enter on a new life, to cast behind us the petty things that encumber our better selves.'[23] Nellie McClung also rejected 'female parasitism' in favour of saving souls for Christ and worked alongside J.S. Woodsworth in Winnipeg's All People's Mission.[24]

The social gospel blurred the line between Church and State since social legislation required state intervention. Following the lead of their men, who turned more and more frequently towards the legislature to remedy an unhealthy social situation, the women soon concluded that they too required a vote, a necessary weapon in the arsenal of every reformer. Since women were commanded to do their share in the reform of the world, they had, not a right, but a duty to vote. Woman's enfranchisement meant simply the consecration of all her capabilities to Christ. Christianity made woman 'a daughter of God' and raised her to such a 'level of opportunity' that a ballot became her due.[25] In this way the social gospel led many women into the suffrage movement.

III

Doubtless the Church's sanction of woman suffrage lent respectability to the movement. In a religious society like Canada, any movement which failed to secure ecclesiastical blessing might well have been suspect. Moreover, the women utilized this 'Trojan horse of respectability' to gain support and approval by offering clergymen the largely titular rank of Honorary President or Honorary Vice-President in the suffrage societies. They also found several genuine reform friends in the Church, notably Adam, Dickie, Symonds, and Hamilton, introduced earlier.

But the Church's endorsement of woman suffrage involved no re-evaluation of its stand on social sex roles. A vote meant simply that woman's religious influence would have a wider field. Even the more radical social gospel ministers advocated a conventional distribution of sexual functions which grew out of the defensive, preservative nature of the social gospel itself. C.W. Gordon, for example, recognized the many new spheres which had attracted women but insisted that 'the impressive fact remains unchallengeable that her natural sphere is that of the Home.'[26] B.F. Austin eulogized marriage and motherhood – 'no height to which vaulting ambition would lead you is more exalted than a mother's seat by the fireside' – and predicted that most women would end up housewives.[27] J.S. Woodsworth, no radical when it came to women's rights, argued that women's presence in the home was essential to assure the physical and moral health of the children. Social order remained his first priority. Since he believed that motherless homes would produce a shiftless, unmanageable future generation, he could not condone the idea of working mothers. In his opinion, the educated class made the best mothers. As a result he berated the trend among educated women to marry later and have fewer children. In fact he condemned the woman's movement because he believed that independence and self-reliance among women could lead to race suicide and the destruction of the family.[28]

The campaign for higher female education, in which the Christian Churches played a leading role, illustrates their narrow, confining attitude towards women. According to many Churchmen, the traditional, frivolous female education encouraged in women a 'listless ennui,' 'a sleep of indifference,' and slavery to 'folly and fashion,'[29] which hardly prepared them for the role of good Christian mother or missionary. To raise feminine ideals, many Protestant ministers founded female academies which offered women a more demanding curriculum than needlepoint and dancing and which emphasized moral and mental discipline and Christian instruction. One such academy, Alexandra College in Belleville, hoped to attract girls already suitably imbued with a strong, Christian devotion by offering an incentive of half fees to the daughters of ministers.[30] The new schools, however, continued to emphasize religion and culture. They restricted women to conventional duties and denied the necessity of professional education for women. According to Albert Carman, the General Superintendent of the Canadian Methodist Church until 1914, women required some intellectual instruction, but he did not expect them to join in professional life.[31] B.F. Austin, a more liberal clergyman, wanted every field of endeavour open to women but even he ranked domestic training as a first priority.

Social circumstances forced the Church to concede that some women might have to work. The increasing proportion of women in urban centres made it difficult for all women to find husbands. However unlikely it might seem, the Church feared that middle-class women in need might resort to the desperate profession of the 'lady of the streets.' The Church's dread of prostitution and venereal disease outweighed its apprehension about women working and, reluctantly, it conceded that in this situation it might be advisable for a woman to know how to support herself.[32]

Independent, self-sufficient women also promised indirectly to improve the quality of middle-class marriage. As things stood, women who faced the alternatives of marriage or poverty chose the former whether or not they felt inclined towards this sphere. Unhappy mothers made poor mothers, poor housewives, and led inevitably to unhappy homes and a rise in the divorce rate. To protect the home, a woman needed at least sufficient training to be able to choose an alternate occupation should she reject marriage.[33] Women's education, therefore, provided a safety-valve for discontents which could, conceivably, undermine the family and subvert the whole social order.

The nationalist fervour of the late nineteenth century strongly influenced Canada's Protestant Churches, particularly the Methodists. They considered it a part of their Christian duty to strengthen and protect the nation from decay. This impulse, rather than a desire to free women from unnatural restraints, lay behind many ostensibly liberal reforms. The discoveries of genetics had revealed the disastrous effects of tight lacing on the womb and of lack of exercise and poor nutrition on a woman's general condition and that of her offspring. Consequently the Churches usually endorsed factory laws, equal pay for equal work, dress reform, and calisthenics for women, all for a single purpose, to improve the race by fostering the health of the mother.

The 'new woman,' therefore, had her usefulness, and the Churches were willing to exploit her fully so long as she knew her place. A more intelligent, better-educated motherhood would produce more intelligent children. Independent women who chose marriage would bring all their energy and dedication to it. The dress reform movement promised to produce healthier offspring. The Methodist minister W.H. Withrow used this logic to justify women's higher education: 'Woman is none the less womanly because she is neither a fool nor a doll ... She is none the better helpmate because she has no sympathy with the studies and employment of her husband. She is none the more charming companion because her thoughts run in a narrow round. She is none the better mother for being engrossed in fashionable folly and frivolity.'[34] Nonetheless, the Churches allowed women greater freedom only if they considered it necessary in the long run for the preservation of order and stability.

IV

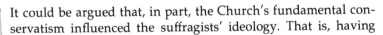

It could be argued that, in part, the Church's fundamental conservatism influenced the suffragists' ideology. That is, having taken up the challenge to serve their Lord, good Christian women would find it difficult to attack the Christian social order. On one level they undertook new responsibilities, but, on another, they dealt only with issues which no one could challenge as being legitimately within their realm – other women, children, the sick and disabled. On these grounds Beverley Harrison has labelled their views 'soft feminism.'[35] As a corollary, it seems logical to conclude that, given the close ties between the social gospel and the woman suffrage movement, this 'soft feminism' contributed to the development of 'maternal feminism.'

A few suffragists chafed under the restrictions imposed by the Churches. Nellie McClung, a temperance woman and a devout Methodist, informed a Methodist Conference in 1914 that it need not send resolutions to the legislatures on behalf of woman suffrage until it cleaned up the Church and gave women a place in the Church courts.[36] In 1916, the President of the Saskatchewan PEFB, Mrs F.A. Lawton, took the same message to the Presbyterians. After the suffrage victory in 1918, Nellie McClung addressed a World Methodist Ecumenical Conference and soundly chided the Church for its unwillingness to break new ground for women, for being 'slow to move, stiff and cold.' 'The Church of Christ should have championed the woman's cause,' she complained. 'It should have led all the reform causes in bringing liberty of soul and freedom of action to women.'[37] Instead, by its die-hard attitude towards feminine equality, she argued, the Church had driven many leading women outside its ranks.

Mrs McClung proved to be correct. The few feminists in the movement who challenged prevailing attitudes towards woman's role became without exception religious rebels, either avowed agnostics like Flora Macdonald Denison or universalists like Mary Crawford in Manitoba and Augusta Stowe-Gullen who declared themselves comfortable in all Churches. Flora Macdonald Denison perhaps best illustrates the feminist-agnostic syndrome. Her unorthodox social attitudes towards marriage and motherhood have already been explored.[38] In a spirit of genuine, undisguised feminism, she refused to acknowledge a man-shaped deity – 'Spirit is free, not personality'[39] – and blamed the Church for woman's continuing subservience. 'The teaching of the Church is at the bottom of woman's slavery,' she declared, 'and until she can recognize the fact and resent the teaching she will remain enslaved.'[40] Mrs Denison had little love for organized religion. She rejected the Puritan God of wrath 'watching mortals and jotting down all the little or big wrong-doings.' She accused the Church of creating the concept of 'sin' to keep men and women in subjection. As a political radical she condemned the organized Church for lavishing on itself 'imposing ceremonies' and 'palatial cathedrals' while it allowed the poor to go hungry.[41]

For all these reasons Mrs Denison abandoned the church and turned to spiritualism. The theory of 'cosmic consciousness,' which maintained that an intelligence existed in and around the world and that particularly sensitive individuals could tune in on it, attracted her interest.[42] In the thinly disguised account of her sister's life, entitled *Mary Melville: The Psychic*, Mrs Denison claimed that her sister possessed this gift and that, after her untimely death at age eighteen, her sister continued to communicate with her. At Bon Echo in southern Ontario, Mrs Denison established a Walt Whitman Club where she drew around her an interesting body of progressive thinkers, including several suffragists who shared her religious views, a fact which suggests the existence of a small subculture within the suffrage movement.[43]

Many more, however, had come to the suffrage movement through the new evangelicalism, and as a result their social message for women was much more moderate. The new social theology aided the suffrage movement by summoning women to assist in creating a healthier social environment and by convincing many men, including many clerics, that votes for women would advance the cause of social Christianity. But the Christian view of the world rested firmly on the family and stressed the priority of woman's maternal duties. As many suffragists were fully committed to spreading the faith and defending Christianity, they made social reform their chief interest and avoided the issue of female equality.

5

Temperate Beginnings

The temperance movement, a movement closely tied to Protestant evangelicalism, provided the single most popular route to suffrage activity for many men and women in Canada. Some 27 per cent of the male leaders belonged to temperance associations. Woman suffrage won their support largely because they believed that enfranchised Anglo-Saxon, Protestant women, the most vocal anti-liquor element in the community, would vote in prohibition. Female prohibitionists, who were equally convinced that women's voices would swing the political balance in favour of prohibitive liquor legislation, constituted almost 25 per cent of the female executive membership. Most of these became suffragists after working for several years in the WCTU. The frustration at seeing their efforts on behalf of prohibition repeatedly defeated in referenda convinced them of the need for a ballot.

The alliance with prohibition helped the suffrage movement in several ways. First, it won the cause many powerful allies and a degree of respectability owing to the popularity of temperance among Canadian reformers and reform politicians. Second, given the broad rural appeal of temperance,[1] it created a valuable link between the predominantly urban suffrage societies and the larger rural constituency. The temperance suffragists, that is, the 25 per cent in the active suffrage societies, tended to be city dwellers themselves (the urban character of the suffrage societies is a constant).[2] But, through the temperance organizations, they had the means to convince rural women of the need for female enfranchisment. And finally, temperance activity gave nine-teenth-century Canadian women their first real political experience. It taught them how to organize, how to persuade and pressure politicians, and showed them the value of a ballot.[3]

Ultimately, however, the temperance suffragists had a taming effect on the suffrage movement. Students of the Canadian campaign for temperance describe it as an essentially defensive impulse on the part of the native, Protestant middle classes, designed to impose their standards on a dissenting community.[4] The men and women who came to suffrage through temperance generally saw woman suffrage as the means to an end, prohibition. Or, more precisely, both woman suffrage and prohibition were the means to a more comprehensive end – a strengthening of the moral and social values in which they believed.[5] To these men and women, women's rights meant little more than that women be given an opportunity to help defend Protestant morality and sobriety. Like the social gospel with which it was closely associated, therefore, temperance strengthened the cautious, conciliatory element in the suffrage movement.

I

The organized temperance movement reached Canada very early in the nineteenth century. Ruth Spence, in her history of *Prohibition in Canada*, claims that in 1827 the community of West River, Pictou County, Nova Scotia, established Canada's first temperance society.[6] One American fraternal association, the Sons of Temperance, came to Nova Scotia in 1847 and arrived a year later in Brockville, Canada West. In 1876 the Dominion Alliance for the Total Suppression of the Liquor Traffic, Canada's most vocal prohibitionist group, was formed. Two important American temperance lodges, the Independent Order of Good Templars and the Royal Templars of Temperance, had a following in Ontario by 1880. Good Christian women, reputed to be virtuous and sober, formed female auxiliaries like the Daughters of Temperance which worked alongside the male associations. These women, however, soon tired of the role of helpmates with no right to speak or vote on resolutions, and started to organize independent, wholly female associations. As early as 1847 a Ladies' Total Abstinence Society appeared in Saint John, New Brunswick.[7] The Woman's Christian Temperance Union (WCTU) soon outstripped all other women's temperance societies.

The Ontario-born Letitia Youmans brought the WCTU to Canada in 1874.[8] WCTU locals spread so quickly that by 1883 there were enough to justify forming a Dominion organization. The base of the movement remained in Ontario, but, by the turn of the century, each province had its own union.[9] By 1915 the WCTU, with over ten thousand members, represented one of the strongest women's reform organizations in Canada.

In the early years of temperance campaigning, the leaders seemed generally confident of their moral authority and their ability to persuade deviants to follow their exhortations. They relied, therefore, upon *voluntary* renunciation of the liquor temptation. The sheer magnitude of the urban problem, however, made pragmatic voluntarists despair. It soon became clear that neither the urban poor nor the plutocrats wished 'to be saved.' Coercion, therefore, replaced suasion and temperance became prohibition.[10] Logically the state became the chief object of their attentions, since the government licensed the liquor trade. Liberal consciences, of course, were still troubled by the implications of 'legislated morality' but did their best to justify and rationalize their position. In the tradition of T.H. Green, the prohibitionists explained that a man who became a slave to drink had renounced his freedom. Prohibition did not end liberty; it offered man a greater freedom, the freedom to become a prosperous, moral, and happy citizen.

With this rationale prohibitionists justified a degree of government intervention and regulation. Few saw beyond using the state as a negative, policing agent, however. Temperance had a strong rural base and its supporters, generally unsophisticated politically, still believed in personal rather than institutional morality. They reluctantly conceded the need to use the government in this instance but hedged at the introduction of other legislation. The temperance suffragists consistently stood to the right in the political spectrum and advocated a very limited state intervention.

The tendency to turn to the legislature to remedy the liquor problem made the women in the movement increasingly aware of their political incapacity. At the local level, under Canada's Scott Act, a community could vote itself 'dry' by securing a three-fifths majority of the eligible voters in a referendum on the issue. The WCTU campaigned for the referenda, but, when the crucial day arrived, the women had to sit back and watch their efforts go down to defeat without even having the chance to record an opinion. This experience turned many WCTU women into suffragists. For example, the President of the Toronto WCTU, Hattie Stevens, asked for full municipal suffrage for married women in 1904 to 'help secure that 60% majority in the Local Option contests.'[11]

Local option became increasingly ineffective in a more mobile, urbanized society where improved transportation made access to 'wet' areas much easier. The prohibitionists, therefore, sought wider restrictions at the provincial and federal levels. In turn the women asked for the provincial and federal vote. By 1891 each WCTU provincial union had established a Franchise Department.[12] Female enfranchisement became a vital means to vote Canada 'dry.'

The vocal and aggressive WCTU campaigns for prohibition converted many temperance men into suffragists as well. As early as 1873 Rev Thomas Webster, an Irish-born minister of Canada's Methodist Episcopal Church, published a volume entitled *Woman, Man's Equal*, which explained why exactly he, a prohibitionist, wanted women to vote: 'I believe, if we are ever to be freed from the rum demon in Canada; if we are ever to secure social purity; if we are ever to occupy the position we should occupy as a Christian country, in working out the country's true destiny and elevating the tone of Eastern immigrants who are to throng our coasts, the rights of citizenship must be given to our women.'[13] Webster was still actively promoting the cause in 1894 when he appropriately became an Honorary member of Manitoba's first Suffrage Club. And it is no coincidence that a prohibition paper, the *Canada Citizen*, contained the first woman suffrage column in Canada, edited by Sarah Curzon in the early 1880s.

Before the end of the century, many of the major male temperance associations had become unreserved sponsors of woman suffrage. The Dominion Alliance, for example, passed a resolution in 1890 endorsing female enfranchisement. Many temperance men actually enlisted in active suffrage societies. The editor of *Canada Citizen*, William Burgess; the organizer of 'Canada's New Party' (a Prohibition Party) in 1888, William W. Munns; artist and Alderman J.W. Bengough and his brother Thomas, both active in the Dominion Alliance; and the Hon George E. Foster, called the 'Neal Dow' of Canada beause of his ceaseless struggle for prohibition – all became aggressive suffragists. Several clergymen who joined suffrage associations also had strong temperance ties; for example, the Rev D.S. Hamilton, a Congregationalist minister who became Honorary President of the Manitoba PEL in 1912, was a Royal Templar and the president of a Temperance League.

The 1894 Ontario plebiscite on prohibition convinced any doubting male prohibitionist of women's commitment to the reform. In this plebiscite, the Ontario Premier, Oliver Mowat, gave Ontario women their first provincial vote, allowing women who qualified for the municipal election – that is, propertied widows and spinsters – to record their opinion on yellow ballots. Fifteen thousand of an eligible forty-four thousand women voted, a substantial turnout given the popular prejudice against women's active involvement in politics. Of these 84.7 per cent favoured prohibition, compared to only 64.2 per cent of the men. Their support for prohibition confirmed the women's worth in the eyes of the male prohibitionists.[14]

The plebiscite also roused the ire of Ontario's married women, who were not allowed a vote simply by virtue of their marriage. The contest, according to May R. Thornley of the Ontario WCTU, proved an 'eye-opener' to hundreds of voteless women 'who toiled unceasingly through the campaign to arouse and interest the favoured few of their sex possessing the ballot,' and who realized, perhaps for the first time, 'the grievous nature of the political disability under which they laboured.'[15]

In the 1898 federal plebiscite on prohibition, no women voted. Smugly, the women blamed the low turnout, only 44 per cent of the eligible electorate, and the slim victory, only 51.3 per cent in favour of prohibition, on their absence. Again in 1902 an Ontario plebiscite failed to attract enough people to justify introducing the legislation and again the women attributed the defeat to the 'futility of attempting to govern a country by less than half of its adult and responsible citizenship.'[16]

In 1905 the Ontario WCTU gave suffrage an important place in its programme. During its annual pilgrimage to the Ontario Provincial Legislature, it insisted on the municipal enfranchisement of all properly qualified women, married and unmarried.[17] In 1906 it decided to make the franchise the 'pivotal point' upon which the success of the temperance movement rested. By 1909 a franchise message had become as much an integral part of every convention as the opening and closing exercises.[18]

II

The Ontario pattern, wedding suffrage to temperance, became a popular strategy across the country, particularly in the Prairies where demographic patterns enhanced the urgency of prohibition. The old Ontario settlers, bringing temperance ideas with them, became the strident advocates of prohibition, their ranks swelled by heavy immigration from the American North-West. The presence of large numbers of Eastern, Central, and Southern Europeans, congregated in isolated settlements which preserved their language, religion, and customs, sharpened the nativist concern and consolidated the prohibitionists.[19]

The WCTU attracted a large, enthusiastic clientele in the West. Following the Ontario precedent, the temperance women soon added female suffrage to their platform. The WCTU actually initiated suffrage activity in the three Prairie Provinces. The Manitoba WCTU campaigned for female enfranchisement from its inauguration in 1877 under the leadership of a former Ontario teacher, Elizabeth Chisholm. Even Manitoba's Icelandic community, the pioneer suffragists in the province, organized an Icelandic chapter of the WCTU in Winnipeg in 1903.[20] In the North-West Territories, the WCTU, initiated in 1904 by Maria G. Craig, a long-standing member of the Quebec WCTU, also led the suffrage battle in the early years.[21]

After 1910, the WCTU consistently canvassed the rural areas in search of suffrage supporters, leaving the cities to the regular suffrage societies and allied women's groups. In this way it filled an important function. It broadened the national base of the suffrage movement and offered proof to the politicians that the city women were not alone in their desire for enfranchisement. In the 1916 petition to the Alberta Legislature, Mrs F. Langford, the Vice-President of the provincial WCTU, claimed credit for 7,000 of the 40,200 signatures, 'collected in the rural districts by the WCTU.'[22]

Owing to the temperance-suffrage association in the public mind, the women found many faithful supporters among Prairie prohibitionists and clergy. They discovered allies in the strongly nativist, staunchly prohibitionist pioneer farmers' groups, in the United Farmers of Alberta and the United Grain Growers' Associations of Saskatchewan and Manitoba. Their alignment with what would later become important political pressure groups was vital to the success of both the prohibition and the woman suffrage movements.[23] The following telegram from J.B. Musselman of the Saskatchewan Grain Growers' Association to the Acting Premier of Saskatchewan, J.A. Calder, in March 1916, on the eve of the provincial concession of the franchise, gives one brief glimpse of the behind-the-scenes politicking and reveals the pressure exerted on behalf of woman suffrage by powerful, prohibitionist allies. Musselman wrote: 'I am instructed by the executive of the Saskatchewan Grain Growers' Association in meeting to memoralize you stating that the body sincerely hopes that provision may be made fully enfranchising the women of Saskatchewan so that they may vote in December next on the referendum on the liquor question.' Calder replied: 'law will be changed at present session *for purpose mentioned.*'[24] While not conclusive, the evidence reinforces the hypothesis that women received the vote primarily because they represented puritanical, moralistic values and not because of the growth of genuine sentiment in favour of sexual equality.

The precise importance of temperance to the suffrage victory is difficult to assess. Temperance, like many other reform causes, became a popular recruiting and training ground for suffragists. It also attempted to bridge the gap between a rural and urban phenomenon. The fact that the twin reforms, female enfran-

'The Women of Manitoba Want to Help Slay the Dragon.'
Grain Growers' Guide, 1 September 1915

chisement and prohibition, were passed almost simultaneously in the Prairies, in British Columbia, and in Ontario suggests their interdependency. But temperance also created enemies whose influence doubtlessly retarded the cause. In the United States, for instance, Carrie Chapman Catt, a national suffrage leader, suggested that the liquor interests made large contributions to anti-suffrage associations.[25] Liquor interests in Sydney, Australia, also financed an anti-suffrage society.[26] In one of her novels, Nellie McClung makes a similar charge, arguing that the brewers were the mainstay of the Roblin Government, the outright opponent of Manitoba suffragists.[27] Although Mrs McClung's claim is oblique and difficult to prove, additional circumstantial evidence exists which implies the existence of a liquor-anti-suffrage alliance. The President of Canada's only anti-suffrage society, Mrs H.D. Warren, was married to a Toronto businessman who in 1902 signed a manifesto against the Prohibition Act, a manifesto Castell Hopkins called the 'last of a vigorous campaign put up by liquor interests and those opposed to Prohibition.'[28] Taken together, this evidence, though scarcely conclusive, suggests that there may have been powerful or rather well-heeled opponents who insidiously worked against woman suffrage because of its close association with prohibition.

III

Although close ties between suffrage and temperance were forged during the reform struggle, the two movements were not coterminous, and their alliance did not evolve without difficulties. Some temperance men and women joined suffrage associations. Yet not every temperance worker became a suffragist, that is, joined a recognized suffrage society. Many who favoured woman suffrage were quite content to work for the female franchise through their own associations. Many others were even unwilling to endorse it at all because of its unpopularity. Letitia Youmans, for example, refused in the early years to become associated with woman suffrage because she feared it might injure the campaign for prohibition: 'So strong was the opposition in Canada to what was commonly called 'women's rights' that I had good reason to believe that, should I advocate the ballot for women in connection with my temperance work, it would most effectively block the way and it was already uphill work for a woman to appear on a public platform.'[29] In 1885, as a propertied widow, Mrs Youmans received a municipal vote; she decided to do her 'duty' but was scarcely enthusiastic about the idea.

Nor did every suffragist belong to the WCTU or male temperance associations, although the majority favoured prohibition. Many, perhaps some 50 to 60 per cent, became suffragists for reasons other than their abhorrence of alcohol. (Their reasons are discussed in a succeeding chapter.) Emily Stowe believed that the association between temperance and the suffrage cause compromised the latter's goals and therefore, disassociated herself from the WCTU. Amelia Yeomans organized the Manitoba Equal Suffrage Club in 1894 for the same reason. Until that date Manitoba suffragists had worked through the Franchise Department of the WCTU. Dr Yeomans demanded that suffrage stand on its own feet so that women who favoured suffrage but opposed prohibition would not be deterred from supporting the former.[30] A few suffragists actually criticized the principle of prohibition. Flora Macdonald Denison called it just 'another form of intemperance.'[31] This was unusual, however, for by 1916 prohibition received verbal support from most suffragists and had become a part of almost every suffrage programme.[32]

The fact that the two movements were not coterminous suggests that the suffragists and temperance advocates differed in several important ways which kept them apart. One student of the American movement, Janet Giele, in a sociology thesis, attempts to explain the basic ideological distinction between a temperance woman and a suffragist. She identifies three stages in women's emancipation – the familial, the extra-familial and the communal – each stage essential to the next.[33] For the most part she sees temperance women predominantly occupied at the familial and extra-familial levels, with their homes, their families, and Church work. Suffrage women on the other hand, she notes, became more involved in broader community activities, particularly in civic reform. Partly because of its rural background, the WCTU, she explains, failed to keep pace with the rapid changes in industrial society and continued to emphasize personal morality when the social problems obviously demanded a more comprehensive approach. Temperance women were less inclined to use the state in other than a purely negative, prohibitory fashion, while the suffragists, generally more sophisticated city women, recognized the need for more serious institutional change. The latter perceived 'the efforts of the temperance groups as somewhat irrelevant to the new social problems around them.'[34] Giele attributes the women's different levels of emancipation, first, to their occupation, and second, to the nature of their education. She discovers that a slightly higher number of suffragists were professionals, lawyers, journalists, while more temperance women were unemployed housewives, and that suffrage women were more likely to have had college and professional training.[35]

In Canada the contrasts are even greater. Based on a sample of nineteen WCTU leaders, only six, or 31 per cent, held an occupation outside the home, compared to 64 per cent of the female suffrage leaders. Both groups of women possessed good educations, indeed exceptional for the period, but the temperance women tended to be graduates of a Ladies' College or a Collegiate Institute, or to have received private tutoring, while most suffragists attended a regular university.[36] Their upbringing undoubtedly influenced their attitudes. Women with a more sophisticated education were more likely to be aware of current political debate and the trend towards greater government intervention. Moreover, women who held jobs in the regular workaday world confronted social problems in a more direct fashion than women whose social experience seldom took them beyond the four walls of their homes.

A second factor, sexual antagonism, distinguished a suffragist from a temperance woman. Suffrage women were clearly more bitter than their temperance allies towards men. On one occasion, in a public letter to the editor of the *Toronto Globe*, Emily Stowe charged that male speakers dominated women's temperance meetings and robbed women of the opportunity to practise public speaking, a situation which left them in a traditionally subservient role. 'Men will never respect us as they ought to,' she protested, 'until we show them that we can get along without them very well.'[37] Letitia Youmans, typical of the more conciliatory, soft-spoken temperance women, approved the dependence upon male speakers and possessed no desire to antagonize her co-workers, 'our brethren who have toiled so long and faithfully in this work.' The WCTU appeared more submissive and patronizing. One member even doubted if Canadian women could ever 'vie with our vice-chancellors, governors, and public men on a platform.'[38]

Social roles once again shaped attitudes. Since temperance women were less likely to be professionals, they confronted little occupational discrimination. Sexual equality, therefore, meant less to them and they displayed a lower degree of antagonism towards men. Temperance women, despite their education, clung much more closely to traditional female roles. The suffragist on the other hand tended to be a more exceptional woman, one who challenged male educational and occupational strongholds. The suggestion, therefore, that women in the WCTU were motivated primarily by sex antagonism, that their reforms constituted an 'outlet for resentments' and an 'oblique attack on the male domination of society,' is disputable.[39] Although the WCTU constituted an exclusively women's organization, its social criticism, its tirade against drugs, social gambling, and impurity differed in no significant respect from male-dominated temperance societies, notably the Dominion Alliance. The men even shared the women's distaste for tobacco, which they blamed for 'weakening the moral, physical, and mental capabilities of the youths of our nation.'[40] Unless we are ready to question the manliness of many temperance men, it is unwise therefore to characterize the WCTU as simply 'attacking anything masculine.'

Temperance men and women shared common interests and common enemies; the battle-line in the movement lay between the classes, not the sexes. Drink was seen as an upper- and lower-class habit, not as a 'distinctively masculine weakness.'[41] The WCTU continually criticized the 'well bred,' 'fashionable,' 'society' ladies for 'taking a fortifier' or serving champagne at their afternoon teas.[42] Nor did they have any illusions about women's, particularly upper-class women's, immunity from other social vices abhorrent to their middle-class tastes – for example, social gambling, which they deemed on the rise among society women.[43]

If, therefore, a degree of sex antagonism distinguished a suffragist from a WCTU woman, how are we to explain the presence of some forty WCTU women in suffrage associations? Some of these women had been transformed into an angrier breed simply by virtue of their impatience with male legislators. Usually they were long-time members of the WCTU who became absolutely convinced that the key to a prohibition victory lay in the women's vote. Without exception, they came from city branches of the WCTU and had absorbed the current political attitudes towards state intervention which naturally increased their desire for voting privileges. More important, the nature of the suffrage agitation had changed. Two processes went on simultaneously.

The influx of temperance women modified the tone of the suffrage societies, making them less aggressive. The more docile the
suffrage movement appeared, the easier it became for less feminist women to join. For the temperance recruits were scarcely
passive members who capitulated to the more outspoken suffragists. They brought their ideas and tactics with them to the
suffrage movement, softening its message.

First, the WCTU women altered the social composition of the
suffrage societies. If we compare the 25 per cent of Canadian
female suffragists with a temperance affiliation to the 75 per cent
who were straight suffragists, we find that 53.3 per cent of the
latter were paid professionals compared to 42.4 per cent of the
temperance suffragists.[44] Moreover, no occupation could be
found for 47.5 per cent of the temperance suffragists, which suggests that they were housewives, compared to only 29.2 per cent
of the straight suffragists.

The straight suffragists also tended to be better educated.
About 35.3 per cent had attended a regular university and held a
BA or better, compared to 22.5 per cent of the temperance suffragists.[45] Only 13.7 per cent of the straight suffragists received
their education in Ladies' Colleges, Collegiate Institutes, or Normal Schools, while 22.5 per cent of the temperance suffragists
graduated from these institutions.

The temperance suffragists also helped alter the priorities of
the suffrage movement and contributed new, moderate arguments in defence of female enfranchisement. They consistently
put prohibition first and saw suffrage primarily as a means to
implement that end. They staked no claim to occupational equality but wished instead to enforce, strengthen, and protect the
traditional female family function, which consisted of raising
children and caring for a home and husband. To temperance
suffragists, 'home protection' constituted the strongest argument
in favour of woman suffrage. Nellie McClung, the best example
of a temperance woman who turned suffragist, went out of her
way to reassure men that enfranchised women would not 'mix
their tricks and lose interest in husband, home, and child.' On
the contrary, she argued, 'the reason for women wanting the
vote is to defend their children, the children they have brought

into the world.'[46] In 1891 Annie Parker, the Superintendent of Franchise for the Dominion WCTU, a devout Protestant, and a member of the DWEA, likened the family and home to a 'miniature state,' a matriarchy ordered by God.[47] Louise McKinney, another temperance suffragist, confirmed that 'Woman's franchise means home protection.'[48]

Politically, although they had acquired some sophistication, the temperance suffragists tended generally to endorse a more limited state intervention than the straight suffragists, primarily of course in the direction of prohibiting alcohol consumption. Temperance suffragists like Mrs Gordon Grant in British Columbia, Letitia Youmans, and Nellie McClung herself were preoccupied with using the government to eliminate boxing, gambling, obscene literature, prostitution – social evils which blatantly challenged the Protestant code of behaviour. Straight suffragists like Emily Stowe and Flora Macdonald Denison expressed a greater interest in more advanced welfare legislation.

The growth of the WCTU faction within the suffrage movement, therefore, curbed and restrained it socially and politically. The growing strength of the temperance representation in the suffrage societies as the century advanced was a symptom of the movement's new conservatism.

IV

The WCTU remained closely allied with the Canadian suffragists throughout the history of the woman's movement. The two groups worked together, led deputations, and collected petitions, right up until victory in 1918. Because the suffrage societies were weak organizationally and numerically themselves, they realized the powerful allies they had in the women of the WCTU and wished to keep their friendship. Moreover, because of the interlocking membership, the two groups appeared to be spokesmen for one and the same cause. In contrast, the American suffrage women tried to disassociate themselves from the WCTU in the period after 1890.[49] For several reasons they no longer wanted or needed temperance support.

Woman suffrage, it seems, became respectable in the United States long before it did in Canada. According to Janet Giele, the turning point was the 1893 Woman's Congress held at the World's Columbian Exposition in Chicago. After that date, suffrage membership doubled, trebled, until in 1910 the American associations boasted some two million members, approximately 3 per cent of the total adult population (over age fourteen).[50] In Canada woman suffrage won acceptance only following the 1910 NCW resolution endorsing it, and at its height the movement could claim no more than ten thousand male and female members or 0.2 per cent of the adult population.

The social composition of the two movements suggests that in the United States woman suffrage had achieved a certain prestige unknown in Canada. From early in its history the American movement contained a good representation of well-to-do philanthropists and reformers. Until 1910 the Canadian movement depended heavily upon women willing to challenge social convention, which explains the large numbers of professionals, especially doctors, in Canada compared to the American suffrage leadership.[51] Between the years 1910 and 1916 the Canadian movement began to attract a large new body of social leaders and married, non-professional society ladies – for example, Lady Drummond, Annie Gardner Brown, the wife of Saskatchewan's Lieutenant-Governor, and Mrs R.R. Jamieson in Alberta, the wife of a former Calgary Mayor.

As suffrage moved up the social ladder, prohibition moved down. At the same time as woman suffrage became popular in the United States, the American WCTU began to lose pre-eminence. Practical city women, it seems, began to doubt if prohibition alone could rectify the grievous social dislocation they observed. Prohibition began to appear narrow and selfish. The woman suffrage movement meanwhile had added to its programme a whole list of broad humanitarian reforms: factory legislation, child welfare, education, prison, and civic reforms, public health and pure food administration. 'Each movement experienced its greatest success in its benevolent period.'[52] The American suffragists, therefore, had no need for a group which they now considered an anachronism. Moreover, the WCTU's antagonizing of the liquor interests sometimes proved more of a liability than a help.

In Canada the WCTU did not outlive its usefulness until well after the 1910 turning point. WCTU membership, in fact, peaked at 10,000 in 1915 and began its decline only after that date, dropping in 1916 to 9,400, and in 1917 to 8,500.[53] Evidence suggests that the WCTU had just begun to lose prominence in the suffrage campaign in 1913, as this WCTU Report indicates: 'Counties which in the past have sent good reports, indicating a live interest (in suffrage) are this year entirely silent, possibly because of local suffrage societies being formed, which may have diverted activity in the department to these channels.'[54]

The WCTU's continuing strength and the slow climb to social prestige by Canadian suffragists can be attributed, in part, to the lower level of industrialization in Canada. As prohibition was designed to reinstate Protestant, Puritan values and redeem a disintegrating social order, it lost popularity only when it began to appear inadequate to these tasks, when the problems of poverty, slums, immorality, disease, ignorance, and irreligion seemed to demand a much broader approach to reform. Canadians had watched with apprehension the explosion of American urban centres, but the plight of the Canadian city did not really come home until well after the turn of the century. Only then did the WCTU's essentially rural philosophy begin to lose meaning. Prohibition no longer seemed the panacea for society's ills. The suffragists, on the other hand, products of the city themselves, recognized the need for a more comprehensive social reform package. They offered a whole series of reforms designed to deal with the problem of the city. Because of the breadth of their programme, although the intentions were basically the same – to tone down the tempo of change and restore order – woman suffrage appeared less selfish and less repressive and more essential to comprehensive societal reform. As a result, it gained popularity at the same time as prohibition on its own lost support.

The connection between prohibition and woman suffrage, like the connection with the social gospel, contributed to the esteem of the woman's movement and to the eventual suffrage victory. The temperance reformers remained a powerful group in early-twentieth-century Canada and their endorsement undoubtedly aided the women politically. The close alliance between the WCTU and the suffragists and the actual overlap in the two memberships also convinced the men in power that the suffragists were really quite an inoffensive group. Woman suffrage ceased to alarm.

At the same time, the rather conservative ideology which lay behind temperance reform gained a strong foothold within the suffrage movement. Temperance suffragists, committed to doing their share towards stabilizing a shaky social structure, generally accepted the traditional allocation of sex roles. In this way they helped make the movement a defender of the social status quo.

6

The Secular Reform Movement

Woman suffrage attracted two types of reformers, those who concentrated upon improving the individual through controlling his behaviour, and those who looked to causes rather than effects in their reform strategy. The temperance suffragists fall into the first category. In the second we find municipal reformers, child welfare reformers, teachers and public school inspectors, juvenile court judges and directors of reformatories, settlement workers, and members of Humane Associations, Welfare Leagues, Parks and Playgrounds Associations, Municipal Ownership, City Improvement and City Planning Leagues. Of those identified, approximately 30 to 35 per cent of both male and female suffragists belonged to such associations. This then constitutes another wing in the movement, the more politically conscious and sophisticated wing, and the wing which one would have expected to hold a more open-minded view of woman's place in the world.

But too much is made of the differences between these approaches. In fact, they shared many of the same goals and aspirations. Both groups came from the same Protestant, Anglo-Saxon élite, heavily dominated by professionals, and were stirred by the same social problems. Both groups bemoaned the 'problem of the city' with its congestion, immorality, disease, and crime. And both were equally eager to Canadianize the foreigner and to impose the Protestant virtues of sobriety, morality, and industry upon the 'masses.' The aims of the two wings of the reform movement were essentially the same – to create a healthy and homogeneous population in Canada and a smooth-running, conflict-free social order.

Means, not ends, differentiated one reformer from the next.[1] The secular reformers found the Church's programme of Sabbatarianism and temperance inefficient and ideologically inadequate. The negative, carping methods of prohibition disturbed them also. They wished to prevent poverty, disease, crime, and immorality by finding and removing their social roots, and were not content simply to patch or punish after the damage had been done. To achieve this goal, they created a 'cradle-to-grave' reform strategy, taking the child at his birth and shaping him into a predictable and productive social unit. Their programme necessitated a greater willingness to use state machinery and the secular suffragists consequently stood left of centre in the political spectrum.

In their search for a comprehensive blueprint for their new social order, the secular reformers latched onto the industrial model. To an extent their approach was schizophrenic. They retained a romantic longing for the simplicity and security of the agrarian past but at the same time admired industrial pragmatism and regimentation. This contradiction coloured every part of their programme. For example, the reformers eulogized the traditional family as the soul and foundation of the social structure and tried to strengthen it against the divisive effects of city life. At the same time, however, they questioned the efficiency of the family as a character-forming influence, and constructed a second line of defence, a complex system of institutions and agencies to perform the task of socialization.

Fundamentally they were traditionalists. The types of arguments they advanced in favour of female enfranchisement sounded very similar to those used by temperance suffragists and social gospellers. Giving the mother a vote, they insisted, would strengthen the family. Women were also needed for their reputed purifying, civilizing, and stabilizing influence. W.F. Maclean, a Toronto municipal reformer, for example, wanted women to vote because they had not been tainted by the 'objectionable' methods of the past.[2] Another urban reform politician,

Aunt Suffragette (to Bachelor Whitney): 'A nice mess you men folks make of running a House. I've come to look after things a little.'
Toronto World, 6 November 1909

James Armstrong, wished to use the moral force of the country's 'industrious and educated Christian womanhood.'[3]

Furthermore, their reform strategy, which focused heavily upon the child, was predicated upon a traditional interpretation of woman's sphere. The logical outcome of their programme, in fact, was the creation of a professional motherhood. Many of the women in the movement who accepted this interpretation managed to escape the injunction themselves by moving into some of the new areas of professional activity opened up by the movement: for example, school medical inspection and social work. But even they were constricted by notions of acceptable female behaviour, and selected occupations which emphasized their nurturing and maternal virtues. While more sophisticated in their approach to social problems, therefore, this group proved equally reticent to challenge the conventional distribution of sex roles. As a result, their premises and many parts of their programme supported the irrefutable conclusion that woman's place, in the main, was in the home.

I

Secular reform had as its ultimate objective the creation of a prosperous and productive Canada, led by a great race of happy and healthy citizens. Each individual would fill a useful role; none would become public charges. The programme was designed to develop within each person the character, the physical vigour, and the mental stability to allow him to play his part fully. The child figured prominently in this model since it provided the best raw material for the new race of well-adjusted citizenry. The motto of the suffragist-sponsored Montreal Child Welfare Exhibition indicates the prestigious place the child held: 'If we are to become a great nation, the well-being of our children must be our first care.'[4] Many of the reforms were child-centred: for example, the child welfare schemes, the 'new' education, and the public health movement.

The high rate of infant mortality aroused particular anxiety. The 1917 Ontario Commission on Unemployment revealed that for every one thousand births in Ontario, 103.7 babies died.[5]

Child care consequently became a patriotic imperative and woman's mothering function correspondingly grew in importance. Mothers' Unions, providing advice on the care and feeding of the young, sprang up across the country.

The abolition of child labour became another popular cause. Doubtless, a humanitarian impulse was at work here, but the reform also had very practical consequences. It was generally believed that factory work ruined a child's mental and physical health and produced long-range weakness and disability for the race. Augusta Stowe-Gullen considered the effects on the race more pernicious than the child's immediate privation. 'Fortunately,' she concluded rather grimly, 'four or five years of this infamous drudgery kills.'[6]

The focus on the young resulted in some instances in freeing women from certain social constraints. For example, contemporary science drew a genetic connection between the child's health and the physical condition of the mother. It was generally agreed that, if women were taught to take as little exercise as possible and to wear styles of clothing which impaired the functioning of their internal organs, the children they bore would either be dead or better off so. As a result, both dress reform and 'physical culture' for women became respectable, but in each case the motivation was racial, not feminist. Similarly, factory women were considered to need special protection, not for their own sake primarily but for the good of the race. The Toronto Suffrage Association included among its list of reasons why women needed the vote 'because millions of women were wage workers and their health and that *of our future citizens* are often endangered by evil working conditions that can only be remedied by legislation.'[7] Granted, in the early days of sweatshop labour some safeguards were necessary, but, because of the reform preoccupation with racial health, the suffragists failed even to consider that protective legislation burdened a working woman with a competitive handicap which made her less employable. Only a very few – for example, Carrie Derick, the leader of the Montreal movement – argued the modern feminist position that restrictive legislation tended to drive women out of work they were well able to perform.[8] Ideally, the majority wanted women out of the factories altogether, which scarcely constituted a plea for equal opportunity.

Since the child's moral health was considered as important as his physical condition, secular reformers consecrated their efforts towards restoring the moral hegemony of the family, considered the primary character-forming influence. All their attempts to raise woman's status, including the suffrage, must be seen in this context. The campaign for Mothers' Pensions demonstrates this philosophy in action. Since the ratio of children raised in orphanages who became social delinquents was exceedingly high, the reformers wished the government to pay widowed and deserted mothers a pension so that they could stay home and look after their offspring. Not only would such action improve the moral character of the next generation, it was argued, but in the long run it would prove cheaper and more efficient than supporting the children, once they matured, in reformatories and prisons. This attitude clearly reflected the conviction that mother was needed at home.

The secular suffragists became some of the strongest campaigners for Mothers' Pensions. Urban life, delinquency, and crime, it seems, worried them far more than a woman's desire for extra-familial occupational opportunities. Rose Henderson, the Montreal suffragist, toured the country on behalf of Mothers' Pensions, and all the suffrage societies included pensions as a plank in their platform.[9] Constance Hamilton's group, the NEFU, actually decided in 1914 to change the emphasis of its campaign from the vote to Mothers' Pensions, 'a greater need in war time.'[10] Secular reform placed a primacy on preserving family ties, 'the greatest source of strength, morality and stability of the social order.'[11]

Unfortunately, the influx of foreigners and the challenges posed by the city to family life made it difficult to guarantee a 'suitable' home life for the majority of children. Susan Houston, in her study of Canadian juvenile delinquency, notes the growing middle-class anxiety at the 'spectacle of an unprecedented number of other people's children surviving – and thriving – unrestrained in society at large.'[12] Circumstances therefore necessitated the construction of a second line of defence, a second chance to mould the child into a worthwhile citizen. 'Not surprisingly,' explains Houston, 'the solution they devised was the creation of surrogate institutions for the lower classes appropriately analogous to middle-class family life.'

The public schools provided the first and potentially most thorough means of transformation. The 'new' education movement of the early twentieth century, very popular among Canadian reformers, had this aim in mind. It encompassed a series of reforms, including compulsory school attendance, kindergartens, and technical education, each in its place designed to produce useful, self-sufficient and dutiful citizens.[13]

Compulsory education was thought to be a necessary protection both for the child and for society. It provided the only means of transforming the immigrant child into a Canadian and prevented ignorant parents from withdrawing their children from school to help supplement the family income. The suffragists, members of an 'intelligentsia' and mostly good liberals, had a supreme confidence in the power of education. Every suffrage society passed a resolution calling for compulsory school attendance.[14]

The kindergarten promised to extricate the child from an 'unhealthy' home environment at the earliest possible date. James Hughes, Toronto's Public School Inspector, actually introduced kindergartens into Ontario. His wife, the former Ada Maureau of New York, another dedicated suffragist, became Ontario's first kindergarten teacher.[15] In New Brunswick, the suffragist Ella B. Hatheway became the President of the Free Kindergarten Association.

The psychology behind the kindergarten movement provides an insight into the suffrage and reform mind. Following the precepts of Froebel and Pestalozzi, the 'new' education favoured giving children a free rein so that the natural creative energies of mankind could find an outlet.[16] The teacher as instructor took a back seat; discipline was frowned upon; children learned from playing and from one another. Typically, Hughes wanted to abolish coercion, to give children more appreciation and less criticism, and to encourage originality.

At the same time, however, the reformers wished the child to evolve in a socially desirable direction. The purpose of the kindergarten, despite all the talk about liberation, was socialization. It aimed to catch a child at a suitably young age and implant social controls within him, thereby making external discipline unnecessary: good Hegelians in this respect, the reformers believed in 'freedom in necessity.' Hughes, for example, saw no real conflict between restraint and freedom. 'Perfect spontaneity,' he argued, 'and complete submission to law are fond lovers.'[17] Although a number of threads and several discrepancies existed within the 'new' education, every branch agreed on this need for moral instruction.[18]

In the schools' off-hours, the parks and playgrounds took over the task of socialization. Even play had to be productive, according to strict Puritan teaching; otherwise the child developed habits of laziness which carried over into adulthood. Mrs John Cox, the Montreal suffragist, traced both delinquency and unemployment to the lack of a playground: 'The boy without a playground is father to the man without a job. The habit of loafing begins in early youth.'[19] The reform was preventive and aimed at discovering a more efficient and more economical social solution to the problems of poverty and crime, as this rhyme suggests:

Give them a chance for innocent sport,
  give them a chance for fun;
Better a playground plot than a court
  and a jail when the harm is done.

Give them a chance; if you stunt them now,
  tomorrow you'll have to pay
A larger bill for a darker ill,
  so give them a chance to play.[20]

Technical education developed in response to another national exigency. The traditional apprenticeship system had disappeared, creating a need for a new type of vocational training.[21] While not enamoured of industrialism, the secular reformers generally realized that it had become a fact of modern life. They believed it preferable, therefore, to train a man than to launch him unprepared into a depersonalized economic system. The 'benevolent' industrialists, meanwhile, in need of a larger, more sophisticated work force, allied themselves to the reformers in this particular cause.

Part of the motivation behind technical and manual training was very practical. Essentially it promised to create a productive, malleable citizenry. Manual training was believed to develop virtues most appropriate in a workman – 'diligence, perseverance, love of order, neatness, dexterity, caution, a love of construction, a respect for the work of men's hands and a contempt for wanton destruction.'[22] Emily Stowe believed that such training provided an efficient and humane way 'to arrest the multiplication and manufacture of criminals.'[23] Avid nationalists, the reformers also wished to equip workmen better in order to compete with foreign rivals.

Technical education had a more idealistic side as well. James Hughes favoured it as a means of utilizing a student's practical talents 'in order to motivate his interest in school and to achieve an all-round development of his character.'[24] But the ethics of industrialism, division of labour, economy of scale, efficiency, and productivity, seem to have been the major impetus behind the movement.

As part of this same philosophy, technical education for boys meant domestic science for girls. After all, in the new society, each individual would fulfil his most natural, most useful role, and everyone agreed that for women this meant the home. Domestic science promised to serve several purposes, each a positive good in the eyes of the reformers. It would increase the comfort of the working-class home, thereby encouraging the men to remain there rather than frequent the brothels and saloons. A content, stable, and sober working class provided the foundation for a great nation. Domestic science also promised, through health and hygiene, to improve the physical condition of the population. Finally, it would strengthen the home by raising the status of housekeeping and counter the trend among ambitious, self-seeking young women to find fulfilment in a career. The pioneer of the home economics movement in Canada, Adelaide Hoodless, was particularly concerned with the havoc the commercial spirit played with the home. According to her it had lured girls away from the 'pleasures and duties of life in the home circle,' and tempted them with greater glory and higher remuneration.[25] A steadily declining marriage rate confirmed her worst fear, that young girls were showing a disinclination to become housewives.[26]

The home economics movement boomed in early-twentieth-century Canada and became one of the reformers' most popular causes. Between 1893 and 1908 domestic science courses were established in the public schools of thirty-two Canadian cities. In 1894 the Hamilton School of Domestic Science opened and in 1900 a Hamilton Normal School for training teachers of Domestic Science was established, with government aid. Saskatchewan had government-sponsored Homemakers' Clubs and domestic science schools formed part of the Agricultural Colleges of Manitoba and Saskatchewan. Macdonald College in Montreal opened a School of Household Science and in 1918 McGill announced a course for women leading to a Bachelor of Household Science.[27]

The majority of the suffragists endorsed the domestic science movement since they shared the ideological preconceptions on which it was based. They agreed that the home had to help in the evolution of the race and that, unless women had a firm foundation in the knowledge of the laws of health, heredity, and hygiene, the race would fail. The Manitoba suffragist and journalist Lillian Beynon Thomas demanded that girls in public school receive a thorough training in domestic science because, in her words, 'the health of the nation is largely in their hands.'[28] Moreover, domestic science gave housekeeping a stamp of professionalization and a certain 'scientific' standing which satisfied some of the women's status needs. In the eyes of the Western suffragist Isobel Graham, home economics had dignified the old-time 'kitchen drudgery' into a delightful and controlled science and changed utterly her conception of its standing among trades.[29]

A certain class bias doubtless motivated many who had difficulty finding domestic servants, particularly trained servants. Canada faced a servant shortage in these years[30] and some suffragists were clearly concerned. Sonia Leathes of the National Equal Franchise Union wrote Elizabeth Smith-Shortt about her unfortunate friend, 'Lady B. of Manchester,' 'who had not been able to get a housemaid for weeks.' 'Everywhere,' she complained, 'the problem is the same.' Mrs Smith-Shortt herself mentioned almost daily her own inability to find efficient help.[31] Domestic science training would clearly ease the problem.[32] On the whole the suffragists may have been disinclined to do housework themselves but they showed little hesitation in conscripting other women to do it for them.

A small feminist minority realized that the whole notion of domestic science restricted women to a purely domestic function. Alice Chown, the Toronto 'militant,' for example, wanted every woman to receive a general Arts education before she chose an area of specialization.[33] The Montreal rebel Carrie Derick also thought it unfair to limit a woman's choice of occupation by making her education centre around cooking and sewing.[34] The social reform majority, however, set the goals for the movement and reinforced the cult of domesticity.

The Home and School Movement, the last phase of the 'new' education, attempted to co-ordinate the efforts of parents and teachers, to forge a 'Holy Alliance' between the two branches of the socialization pincer. It hoped to humanize the impersonal education process and to provide the teachers with vital information about the home life of their charges. Thereby it completed the circle and guaranteed that the child which emerged from the system fitted easily into his assigned slot in society. Secular suffragists figured prominently in parent-teacher societies. James Hughes' Central Arts Leagues were forerunners of the Home and School Association. Another Toronto suffragist, Ada C. Courtice, the wife of Rev A.C. Courtice, editor of the *Christian Guardian*, founded the first branch of the Ontario Home and School Association in 1916.[35]

II

All the reforms considered so far aimed at improving the *next* generation through training and educating the young. But the reformers still had to deal with the visible social failures of their own era. Their programme was essentially future-oriented, but they still managed to keep an eye on the present. They concentrated their efforts on redeeming the young and first offenders. To these cases they applied similar techniques of social regeneration, specifically technical training courses. Three suffragists at least dedicated themselves to rescuing juvenile delinquents. Mrs R.R. Jamieson in Saskatchewan and Helen Gregory MacGill in British Columbia became Juvenile Court Judges while Rose Henderson in Montreal served as a Probation Officer. [36]

The female suffragists paid special attention to the problems of female offenders. They demanded the segregation of male and female prisoners, the introduction of policewomen, and separate courts for women. This woman-centred side of their programme ought not to be ignored. But these causes also found wide acceptance in the reforming community at large, and the motives seem to have been moralistic rather than feminist.

Hardened criminals faced segregation, in order to prevent contamination of the first offender. However, even they were offered a whole series of humanitarian reforms designed to make prison life more bearable – the abolition of strait-jackets, cold showers, and striped suits. [37] A definite humanist impulse is also revealed in the condemnation of capital punishment and the recommendation of rehabilitation farms.

Many secular suffragists looked for the reasons for crime in the mental condition of the perpetrators. Social surveys and early psychological studies – for example, R.G. Dugdale's famous study of the Jukes family in 1874 – traced a direct link between feeble-mindedness and crime. Lillian Beynon Thomas blamed feeble-mindedness for 51 per cent of all prostitution, though it is difficult to see how she arrived at this figure. [38] Carrie Derick, an extremist when it came to race purity, considered alcoholism, venereal disease, and poverty all the results of mental deficiency. [39] Contemporary notions of heredity convinced her that sterilization provided the only real protection for the future. Most suffragists stopped well short of this extreme position, content with compulsory institutionalization, segregation of the sexes, immigration restriction based on physical and mental examination prior to embarkation, and compulsory medical certificates before marriage proving mental as well as physical health.[40]

Physical, particularly infectious, diseases like smallpox, tuberculosis, and venereal disease presented a serious problem as well. Compulsory vaccination solved the first of these; the remaining two proved more troublesome. Still retaining their preventive orientation, the reformers wished to root these problems out at their source. Because poor ventilation and inadequate nutrition seemed tied to tuberculosis, they campaigned to improve the living and working conditions of the poor. The 'purity crusade,' discussed at length in the next chapter, rested on the premise that immorality produced venereal disease.

Persons who had already contracted infectious illnesses could either be treated, if a cure existed, or segregated, to prevent transmission to others. In order to treat disease, however, it had first to be detected. Compulsory medical inspection of school children provided one means of screening the population for illness, and it therefore appears in every suffrage platform. Carrie Derick actually supported compulsory school attendance primarily because it guaranteed that all children were subjected to medical inspection.[41]

The success of some of their proposed reforms brought occupational rewards to many suffragists. Mary Crawford, President of the Manitoba Political Equality League, for example, led the campaign on behalf of compulsory medical inspection of school children and then proceeded to become medical inspector of Manitoba's public schools.[42] Our juvenile court judges and probation officers also found jobs as an outcome of the reforms they sponsored. Only a cynic would suggest a conscious, premeditated connection, but perhaps at a deeper psychological level there is a causal link. Christopher Lasch has suggested that American suffragists and urban reformers belonged to an intellectual élite which was trying to carve out a sphere of influence for itself in a crass, materialistic, anti-intellectual bourgeois culture.[43] The reforms they supported, public health, education, child welfare, says Lasch, provided them with two kinds of security: occupational, since the reforms placed a premium on their services, and psychological, since they gave them a position of respect in the community. The same observation might apply equally to Canada, particularly given the higher number of professionals in the Canadian suffrage movement.

The occupational rewards offered to women tended to be restricted, however. In most instances they were shunted off into specialized job ghettos which seemed to suit their maternal instincts.[44] Women doctors, for example, became medical school inspectors, or specialists in women's or children's diseases. The lifting of the sex bar seduced the women to an extent and they willingly moved into areas set aside for them. Some became preoccupied with defending their newly won professional status and failed to realize the limitations still imposed on their activities.[45] Professionalization had this effect at a more general level as well, for once the professionals found their niche, they tended to become complacent and lost much of their reforming zeal.[46]

III

Secular suffragists were usually less hesitant than temperance suffragists to call upon the state to implement their reforms. Compulsory schooling, factory legislation, Mothers' Pensions, compulsory medical inspection, compulsory vaccination – all depended upon the intervention of the state in the everyday life of the community. Although this hardly made them socialists, a positive attitude towards the usefulness of state machinery definitely characterized this side of the movement.

The state was asked to intervene in other areas considered vital to the community. For example, the reformers wished the government rather than some independent business cartel to control natural monopolies like water and electricity. Several suffragists joined in the municipal ownership movement. Emily Stowe, her daughter, Augusta Stowe-Gullen, and a third Toronto suffragist, Jessie Semple, organized a Women's Citizens' Association in 1895 to campaign for a municipal aqueduct.[47] Later, in 1907, Flora Macdonald Denison worked for the creation of Ontario Hydro-Electric.[48] In 1913 the Montreal Suffrage Association tried to have the Public Utilities Commission take over the city's transport system, to punish the independent Montreal

Tramway Company for refusing to reduce fares.[49] The suffrage societies generally included a plank in their platform asking for public ownership of natural monopolies such as railways, telephones, and telegraph services, especially in the West where the Eastern monopolies posed a particular danger.[50]

The reformers became suspicious whenever profit and the public good seemed in conflict and were willing to use the government to reduce that conflict. For example, in the food adulteration scandals at the turn of the century, they called upon government inspectors to clamp down on faulty weights and measures, price fixing, and impure additives. Some of the suffragists confronted the food profiteers with an early form of consumer power. They realized that women controlled the larger part of the purchasing dollar and could, if organized, use it to force manufacturers to live up to recognized health standards. Edmonton's suffragists organized a Consumers' League to crusade against overcharging and underweighing. A Calgary suffragist, Mrs E.P. Newhall, founded the Calgary Consumers' League.[51] This interesting innovation introduced many women to the world of political power blocs and lobbies, and convinced them of their need for a ballot. 'Consumer power' also brought women together and allowed them to verbalize their discontents. But at the same time the reform focused upon the organization of housewives within the home and involved no fundamental change in woman's role.

Suffragists were also very active in the city planning movement, another attempt to cope with industrial growth and urban sprawl. Urban reformers advocated planned development. They instituted housing commissions, roads commissions, and parks commissions to set aside areas for public recreation. The Montreal suffragist James Alfred Dale, Professor of Education at McGill, sat on the executives of the City Improvement League, the City Planning Committee, and the Montreal Parks and Playgrounds Association.[52] In New Brunswick, Mabel Peters, Vice-President of the New Brunswick Suffrage Association, was said to be responsible for the supervised playgrounds movement. In 1902 she convened the NCW Committee on Supervised Playgrounds.[53]

'Canada Needs a "Clean-up" Week.'
Grain Growers' Guide, 12 May 1915

The women involved in urban reform paid partcular attention to the aesthetic side of the problem. Manitoba suffragists organized a Women's Civic League in 1914 which worked for the preservation of 'Winnipeg the Beautiful.'[54] Another suffragist, Mrs J.O. Perry, headed the campaign by the Vancouver Beautiful Association for the eradication of 'can-strewn alleys, untidy vacant lots, unsightly bill boards and the smoke nuisance.'[55] Women still found it easier to play the part of the nation's housekeepers.

Many of these reforms – public ownership, anti-adulteration crusades, and city planning – had an anti-business tinge to them. But, as Robert Wiebe has pointed out, businessmen frequently promoted these reforms themselves.[56] In particular, city planning, which has been called 'businessmen's socialism,' did not restrain trade but provided it with conditions conducive to its growth, 'expansion, efficiency, economy and enterprise.'[57] Many of Montreal's great commercial bodies – for example, the Royal Architectural Society and the Board of Trade – endorsed the creation of a Metropolitan Parks Commission in 1909.[58] Turn-of-the-century reformers were therefore not necessarily enemies of the business community. This hypothesis is supported by the fact that several suffragists worked in the business world and others were married to businessmen, although they scarcely constituted a majority in the movement.

The same desire for efficiency which lay behind city planning led some municipal reformers to support the creation of boards of experts to supervise the scheme. Instances of political graft and corruption had disillusioned many. They were therefore prepared to institute a body of controllers which would stand above the electorate and operate in a businesslike manner. Very few recognized the threat to democracy inherent in such a recommendation.[59]

This willingness to surrender control into the hands of administrative experts is a symptom of a spiritual malaise in the movement, revealed in the soul-searching of several suffragists. At one level those involved in secular reform were humanitarians, genuinely distressed by the condition of the poor. The Toronto suffragist Alice Chown, who became involved in many anti-poverty activities, explained that she turned to reform simply because she could not tolerate the existence of poverty: 'It is always the poor that I see ... I am ill at ease with every luxury I allow myself.'[60] But the reformers had difficulty surmounting a paternalistic, patronizing attitude towards the disadvantaged. In the settlements, homes run by professors and college students in impoverished neighbourhoods, Chown found a 'holier than thou' feeling. Even she confessed to finding it difficult to overcome a certain class snobbery.[61] Carrie Derick, the founder of the Montreal Girls' Club which later became the McGill University Settlement, had constantly to warn college girls who worked there not to regard working women as 'providential material for dispassionate study.'[62] The women were so plagued by the desire to do good and the inability to do so without assuming a superior air that Derick suggested turning over all philanthropy to an independent, objective body, the government. The service would be both efficient, she explained, and detached, hence injuring no one's feelings.

The problem of the city had simply become too large for the reformers to handle. They saw the continuing decline of familial authority and the general failure of their efforts to stop it. Increasingly, they turned to secondary institutions and agencies, to schools, social work centres, and reformatories. And, increasingly, they asked the government to supervise these agencies and co-ordinate services. Many, of course, followed their reform career to its professional conclusion and became government employees. Many more took the opportunity to relieve themselves of a growing burden and retired in favour of the new Welfare State. Unfortunately, they failed to consider the danger and deficiency of impersonal, administrative charity.

The female suffragists meanwhile found in the secular reform movement usefulness, recognition, and power among prestigious allies. Some few even found themselves careers. Secular reform also raised homemaking to the rank of profession and thus satisfied the homemaker's status needs. For the majority of women, however, the message remained the same as that promoted by the temperance suffragists, women's duty to stay within and defend the home. In fact, secular reform made this duty more sacrosanct than ever before.

7

Race Regeneration, Evolution, and Social Purity

The ideology of late-nineteenth- and early-twentieth-century reform in Canada, as expressed in the suffrage movement, was complex. The movement included prohibitionists and municipal reformers. Attitudes towards the government ranged from the moderate interventionism of the COS to a more complete State Welfarism. One unifying theme, however, underlay the entire movement and made sense of its diverse strands – a concern for the future of the Anglo-Saxon race. Most of the reforms in some way aimed at strengthening and preserving this kin-group against internal weaknesses and external threats. Two areas in particular caused concern: the declining birth rate, especially among the 'better sort' of people, and the pollution of the race by infectious diseases like tuberculosis and venereal disease.

A closer look at these two overriding preoccupations demonstrates convincingly that the reform ideology restricted the role options of women who believed in it. Concern about the falling birth rate, for example, caused them to place a premium on woman's role as procreator. Anxiety about the health of the population made her nurturing functions seem more important than any extra-maternal occupations she might take up. The problem of venereal disease was countered by attempts to reinforce a Protestant, Puritan morality which emphasized woman's asexuality and made prospects of female sexual liberation unlikely. This is not to suggest that male reformers *imposed* a constricting programme upon the women in the movement, but that, as members of the same social élite, the women shared the same fears and generally favoured the same reforms as the men.

I

Several studies of late Victorian and Edwardian society point to the fact that the English-speaking, Anglo-Saxon communities in Britain, her colonies, and the United States felt defensive in this period.[1] The number of recruits for the Boer War rejected on the grounds of physical incapacity caused a public scandal in England. In reaction, a whole series of reforms from factory legislation to milk for school children, reforms Bernard Semmel labels 'social-imperialism,' were introduced in order to upgrade the health of the population.[2]

The threat of a declining birth rate seemed even more serious. The old Malthusian fear that too many people were being born gave way to the fear that the English population had stopped growing. The problem was not simply numbers, though it was frequently expressed in these terms. The real danger was that the 'best stock' were being outbred by the 'unfit.' Studies, for example, revealed an increasing number of feeble-minded in the population.[3]

These fears travelled easily across the ocean. Canada's social élite considered itself part of this larger collectivity, labelled at times the 'British Empire,' at times the 'Anglo-Saxon race.' Some reformers believed that Canada could become a regenerative force within the Empire, the new 'City Upon a Hill,' 'favoured of God,' 'free from the blighting evils that afflict and torment older lands.'[4] Consequently, much of the reform programme aimed at improving the calibre of tomorrow's citizens.

The idea of evolution attracted the reformers' interest since it seemed to suggest that the human race was moving forward and that all they had to do was to harness the process. Unfortunately, scientists could not agree upon the mechanism by which evolution took place, making it difficult to design a reform strategy. Two contrary theories were developed. Environmentalism, traceable to Jean-Baptiste de Lamarck, maintained that a modification in the environment produced physical and mental changes in a person which were transmitted to the next generation. The opposing school of thought, labelled 'eugenics' by its founder, Francis Galton, placed emphasis on nature, that is, genetic composition, rather than on nurture.[5]

The two schools offered different solutions to the race degeneration and race suicide problems. Lamarckians and neo-Lamarckians, because they believed in the inheritance of acquired characteristics, recommended ameliorative legislation to improve the living and working conditions of underprivileged groups. According to their hypothesis this would produce higher types in the future. The simple answer to the birth-rate dilemma, according to environmentalists, lay in reducing the infant death rate by upgrading the standard of living generally. Eugenists, on the other hand, discounted reforms which modified the environment since they did not feel that such changes in any way altered genetic structure. They insisted that the only way to improve the race was through selective breeding and to this end recommended legislation which prevented the unfit from breeding and which encouraged the fit to have more children.

While it seems clear from studies of the movement elsewhere that reformers could and did support both programmes,[6] the suffragists in the main tended to place more faith in environment than genes. Emily Stowe, for example, blamed the environment for the production of the criminal. She predicted happy results if the money expended on negative, punitive measures, 'to house, watch, detect, and punish our criminals,' were used in the kindly, positive care and education of the young of that group.[7] Flora Macdonald Denison similarly believed that 'environment of a bad social condition produced social failures.'[8] Most reforms in the suffrage platform (factory legislation, compulsory education, city planning, health and hygiene, temperance, prison reform, pure food laws) were 'euthenist,' in contradistinction to eugenist,[9] and aimed at improving the living and working conditions of the poor.

Strict eugenists in the movement were few. Only Carrie Derick, a student in McGill's Botanical Department between 1887 and 1890, and later a Professor of Evolution and Genetics, championed the direct application of scientific principles to human conditions. That is, she believed that the struggle for existence ought to be allowed to proceed unrestrained, so that the truly fittest would survive. She preferred a 'spirit of indifference' to the 'happy feeling' that education, pure air, good housing, proper food, and short hours of work might bring about a permanent improvement in people.[10]

Derick was obviously in a minority since most suffragists were committed to exactly these types of reform. And because these people needed to believe that their efforts would bear fruit in the future, they were unlikely to favour a eugenic approach. Eugenics challenged the usefulness of their activities and, even worse, suggested that reforms of this nature might actually contribute to the deterioration of the race by preserving weak specimens.[11] Ethel Hurlbatt, a vocal member of the Montreal Suffrage Association and Warden of McGill's Royal Victoria College in 1907, understood the dilemma posed by eugenics and the way in which it challenged the basic assumptions of the suffragists' reform programme:

Is degeneracy in every form to be attributed to poverty, bad housing, unhealthy trades, drinking, industrial occupations of women and other direct and indirect environmental influences on offspring? Can we, by education, by legislation, by social effort change the environmental conditions and raise the race to a markedly higher standard of physique and mentality? Or is social reform really incapable of effecting any substantial change, nay by lessening the selection death rate, may it not contribute to emphasizing the very evils it was intended to lessen? ...

Through investigations they [eugenists] show that improvement in social conditions will not compensate for bad hereditary influences; that the problem of physical and mental degeneration cannot be solved by preventing mothers from working, by closing public houses, by erecting model dwellings; that the only way to keep a nation strong mentally and physically is to see that each new generation is derived from the fitter members of the generation before.[12]

While the majority rejected this conclusion, which would very quickly have made most of their reforms seem futile, they did incorporate some eugenic theory into their programme. The

suggestion that the race was breeding to its lowest common denominator was too frightening to ignore. As a result, many
suffragists admitted that environmental reform had a limited
effect on *mental* capacity and therefore it might be necessary to
regulate the breeding of the retarded. One Western woman
wanted special industrial farms, segregation of the sexes, and in
some cases sterilization to keep the feeble-minded from multiplying.[13] In the East, Constance Hamilton, President of the NEFU,
included drunkards among the unsalvageable. She recommended keeping them under restraint rather than leaving alco-
holic mothers 'free to fill cradles with degenerate offspring.'[14]

Clearly, given the early-twentieth-century adulation of science, the new discoveries about heredity proved difficult to dis-
count. But equally, if the attitudes of the suffragists are indicative
of the larger reform movement, the predominant feeling was
that man could still affect his future. The 'cradle-to-grave' reform strategy rested upon this assumption. Dr Peter Bryce,
President of the Canadian Purity Education Association, demonstrated this ability to integrate some eugenic arguments without
abandoning a basically environmental approach. To control the
spread of hereditary weakness, he recommended stricter government regulation of marriage and the removal of the feeble-
minded to state-supported homes. But he still insisted upon the
need for a 'sanitary environment,' improved housing, lessening
of overcrowding, a reduction in local taxation and child labour,
and lower costs for food and land. Bryce considered the two
processes complementary. On the one hand the 'Law of Heredity' doomed men and women to carry their ancestral physical
structure and character with them; on the other, the 'Gospel of
Heredity' mitigated the doom, providing in environment the
'potentialities of almost infinite improvement.'[15]

II

The female suffragists had other, very practical reasons for pre-
ferring environmentalism to eugenics. Environmentalism provided much greater scope for women to contribute actively to
the creation of the new race, while eugenics reduced the mater-

nal function to a mere biological capacity. According to eugenic theory, the principal cause of racial decay was that people with hereditary defects were multiplying faster than those with desirable traits. This trend was attributed in part to the reluctance of intelligent women to stay home and have babies. Eugenists accused these women of abandoning their racial duty and used statistics which revealed a lower marriage and birth rate among college women to prove their case.[16] Francis Galton, the well-known founder of eugenics, was quite prepared to see this duty forced upon them. 'If child-bearing women must be intellectually handicapped,' he explained, 'then the penalty to be paid for race predominance is the subjection of women.'[17]

This conclusion obviously raised a real dilemma for the female suffragists. Since most were well educated and since they belonged to the very social élite that was concerned about the future of the race, what could they say to those who accused them of not doing their share? Ethel Hurlbatt did some soul-searching over the issue: 'If the philanthropists are right, there is no doubt that college women are contributing their share to movements which will secure better physical and moral conditions for the race. If the eugenists are right, are college women? Do college women maintain the same standard of physical efficiency as their less educated sisters? Do they as readily marry? Do they bring into the world as many children?'[18] She could only hope that the 'philanthropists' (or environmentalists) were right, since that made women's contributions to the reform effort as important as their breeding function.

Environmentalism also allowed women to demand a more active and freer life-style on the grounds that improvements in woman's physical and mental fitness today could be transferred to her offspring tomorrow. The 'frail vessel' consequently fell into disrepute. Dr Edward Playter, an Ottawa reformer, announced that 'the age for regarding as fashionable and popular delicate women and girls is past.'[19] It had become 'a woman's duty to be well.'[20] As a result, more and more educators began to press for physical education facilities for girls in order to improve the health of future mothers. All the new women's colleges in the period, such as the Royal Victoria College in Montreal, had large recreation rooms where women learned calisthenics. In a similar manner, environmentalism helped women who wished to reform clothing fashions. The argument that the 'corset curse' might damage the womb or its occupant gave dress reform a patriotic flavour.[21]

Environmentalism could also be used to justify women's higher education. Many people, including many clerics, had begun to criticize the traditional academy education which concentrated on needlework, dancing, and languages, on the grounds that it produced a flighty and frivolous woman. One champion of women's higher education, McGill's Principal William Dawson, insisted that the mental discipline of future wives and mothers had to be improved since the children were in their care all day.[22] This then was the answer to Galton who was willing to restrict women's intellectual development to guarantee their fecundity.

Environmentalism clearly suited the purposes of the female suffragists better than eugenics, since they wished to join the intellectual meritocracy and wanted woman's nurturing duties to acquire more importance. But in some ways environmentalism was as limiting as eugenics. True, it allowed woman a greater scope for activity, but within a very limited domain. It justified the pursuits of the female reformers, but they constituted a small élite within the general female population. It also allowed women to break free of certain parts of Victorian convention, in particular the restraints on exercise and education. But each reform still aimed at improving woman's maternal capacity and in no serious way challenged traditional sex roles. Exercise would produce healthier mothers; higher education would produce more intelligent mothers. The suffragists sensibly aligned themselves with a theory which at least promoted women above the level of breeding stock, but the obsession with race regeneration meant that woman's maternal functions remained her chief contribution to the world.

The domestic science issue demonstrates how environmentalism restricted women's role options.[23] Those who promoted domestic science training usually argued that women needed to know how to feed and care for their children properly in order for the race to improve. Only a small feminist minority realized

that such training restricted women to a purely domestic function. Similarly, the arguments in favour of factory legislation
were essentially racial.[24] That is, the women had to be kept
healthy to protect their offspring. Ideally, the majority of suffragists would have preferred to terminate factory work for women
because of the threat it posed to their health and the health of
their progeny. A racial concern clearly closed more options than
it opened.

III

One particular threat to the health of the race, venereal disease, attracted a growing amount of attention at the beginning of
the twentieth century. Syphilis and gonorrhea had reportedly
reached staggering proportions. Charles Hastings, Toronto's
public health inspector, quoted the ominous findings of the 1901
New York State Commission of Seven which concluded that one
New Yorker in five had venereal disease.[25] Canadian reformers
often looked to the United States to forecast their future and
clearly the future looked grim. The Alberta reformer Emily
Murphy indicated the deteriorating situation in Canada. She
found that one in three prisoners in Alberta's Provincial jail had
to be treated for syphilis or gonorrhea.[26]

The anticipated impact of these diseases on future generations
magnified the danger they posed. In 1905 Fritz Schaudinn and
Erick Hoffman discovered the spirochete which caused syphilis
and proved that it could be transmitted from an infected mother
to an unborn baby.[27] Subsequent studies claimed that syphilis
produced other afflictions including insanity, paralysis, blindness, deformity, and sterility in the victim and in the victim's
offspring. Lillian Beynon Thomas blamed syphilis for 50 per cent
of all mental deficiency.[28] Dr Hastings attributed to gonorrheal
infection 20 to 25 per cent of all blindness, 17 to 25 per cent of all
sterility, and 60 to 80 per cent of all miscarriages.[29]

More frightening still, no easy cure was available. One treatment for syphilis, doses of mercury, used as early as 1497, killed
many patients and made the medicine as dangerous as the disease. Arsphenamine or salvarsan, a derivative of arsenic deve-

loped in 1910, proved more successful, but a clinical cure still required repeated injections over a period of one and a half years.[30] Some later stages of syphilis proved refractory to all forms of therapy, and no effective treatment was available for gonorrhea until the 1940s.[31]

Municipal authorities in Europe, Britain, and some American cities had tried to control the problem by segregating prostitutes, reputedly the chief carriers of the disease, and subjecting them to compulsory medical inspection. Between 1864 and 1869, Britain had Contagious Diseases Acts which allowed the police to pick up and have examined any woman suspected of being a prostitute, and if she were found to be infected, to detain her in hospital until she was pronounced cured.[32] A group of reformers headed by Josephine Butler attacked this legislation on the grounds that it denied women's civil liberties and constituted state sanction of moral evil. The idea of regulation was doomed for an even more practical reason, however: it failed to work. Prostitution simply went underground and venereal disease statistics rose.[33]

Other attempts were made to prevent the 'fallen' from transmitting the disease. In 1912 the Canadian Methodist Church demanded that all cases of venereal disease be reported to Medical Health Officers, and that no one be granted a marriage licence until he or she could produce a medical certificate that established freedom from venereal disease.[34] Dr Hastings suggested the provision of public laboratories where Wasserman tests (discovered in 1906) could be carried out.[35] In 1918 Mary McCallum, then women's editor for the *Grain Growers' Guide*, recommended the strictest and closest quarantine of venereal disease patients.[36]

Retaining the preventive orientation of social reform, many people were not satisfied with these post hoc remedies and decided instead to launch a crusade for the general reformation of the nation's morals as a means of rooting the evil out at its source. Several organizations specifically dedicated to purity reform appeared. For example, between 1906 and 1915, a Purity Education Association, staffed mainly by doctors, operated out of Toronto.[37] A second group, a National Council for the Abolition of the White Slave Traffic, founded in 1912, fought against the international trade in prostitutes. Beyond this, social purity operated as a subsidiary theme in many associations created to fight other evils. The WCTU, for example, had committees for press and literature censorship, as well as committees dedicated to eliminating the white slave traffic and the 'social evil' (prostitution).[38] In fact, according to David Pivar, purity reform underlay the entire reform movement, providing the 'moral cement that gave cohesiveness to otherwise disassociated reforms.'[39] The purity issue acquired this overriding importance for several reasons. Venereal disease clearly presented a major challenge to racial health. Moreover, the spread of prostitution seemed to undermine the family structure and Puritan morality. In brief, impurity challenged the values, authority, and goals of the Protestant social élite.

Purity reformers adopted several strategies. Some people were content to concentrate upon censorship and the restricting of information. Others took the opposite tack and recommended a type of sex education which would encourage continence and discourage sexual activity. A *Self and Sex* series, published in the United States between 1900 and 1915 and enumerating the frightful consequences of venereal disease, became equally popular in Canada.[40] The WCTU and the evangelical Churches even hired purity reformers like Beatrice Brigden, William Lund Clark, and Arthur W. Beall to tour the schools and warn youngsters about the effects of sexual promiscuity.[41]

An even more comprehensive approach recommended raising the status of good Christian women on the grounds that, given the power, they could help make the nation pure. The Victorian female was popularly believed to be asexual, while men were generally labelled the 'promiscuous sex.' A double standard of morality had previously allowed the men to 'sow their wild oats' while the women protected the hearth. Now, it seemed, this double standard had to be overthrown for the sake of the race. Dr Hastings felt it most important to blot out the 'physiological fallacy of sexual necessity for men.'[42] Since female enfranchisement promised to raise women's status and to give them a direct voice in affecting legislation, many purity reformers decided that this was the shortest and best route to the moral regeneration they desired. In fact, almost every male reformer who became a suffragist would have listed as his most important reason for doing so this conviction that women would clean up society morally and, as a direct consequence, physically.

The women in the movement shared this conviction. They personally upheld a strict Victorian code of morality and felt that, given greater influence, they could impose this code on society at large. Emily Stowe approved of the 'anti-sex' sex education which taught the young 'all the consequences of the transgression.'[43] In a similar vein, Amelia Yeomans issued a foreboding pamphlet entitled 'Warning Words,' which recounted all the dire effects of venereal disease. Lillian Beynon Thomas advised women to wear modest dress in order to curb 'animal desire.'[44] Alice Chown, the Toronto feminist, wished to limit sex relations to purposes of reproduction.[45]

The suffrage programmes reveal a preoccupation with the purity issue. Several items aimed directly at ending the prostitution and white slave trades. The plea that the age of consent be raised to age twenty-one, for example, was designed primarily to protect young girls from the white slave traders. Every suffrage society also demanded that proprietors be held responsible for the order and respectability of their houses, an attack against the brothel keepers.[46] Flora Macdonald Denison was even willing to violate cherished civil liberties to end prostitution. She wanted the city to be divided into districts each having an officer with the power to go into any home and find out about its inmates.[47]

But the female suffragists intended to do more than simply clamp down on the criminals; they had hopes of reforming the entire male population. The purity issue aroused them to display a certain degree of sex antagonism, uniting them in a sisterhood of sorts against men. It angered them, for example, that the prostitute consistently played the villain while the man got off with a nominal fine.[48] In their opinion the prostitute was probably less guilty since she often 'fell' through hunger or was driven into sin because 'some man' paid her starvation wages.[49] Flora Macdonald Denison bemoaned the fact that 'hundreds of *our sisters* are forced to live lives of shame to keep body and soul together.'[50] Lillian Beynon Thomas wished to subject the men to equal mortification by having the names of those found in houses in the red light district published in newspapers.[51]

Other victims of 'male licentiousness' aroused sympathy also. The unwed mother, for example, was not held responsible for her condition. Agnes Chesley, women's editor for the *Montreal Star*, recommended that such women be treated with infinite compassion since 'If a girl goes astray, the fault must be looked for in her heritage from her parents, her environment and, above all, in her upbringing.'[52] Existing parental custody laws made the father the sole legal guardian of legitimate offspring but left the illegitimate child the sole responsibility of its mother, suggesting that she was somehow guilty. Nellie McClung pointed to the injustice of this situation: 'If a child is a treasure in a married happy home and clouds arise and a separation follows, who gets the child? The father! But who gets the illegitimate child that bears the brand of shame? The poor unfortunate mother ...'[53] Equal parental rights over legitimate and illegitimate children became a popular cause among suffragists.

The move to liberalize divorce laws aimed at freeing women from sexual exploitation. The suffragists objected most strongly to the clause which allowed a man a divorce on the grounds of adultery but which denied such a right to a woman unless she was forced to cohabit with her husband's mistress.[54] The option of divorce meant a woman no longer had to tolerate her husband's sexual whims, his brutality, or his promiscuity.

According to John and Robin Haller, purity reform had a particular appeal for Victorian feminists since it offered them a kind of sexual freedom. The Hallers argue that contemporary social values would not countenance female promiscuity, and, as a result, the women had to deny their sexuality in an effort to keep from being considered or treated as sex objects.[55] Their prudery was a mask that conveniently hid the more 'radical' effort to achieve freedom of person. Michael Bliss similarly links the movement for sexual repression to the movement to liberate women – 'often, indeed, to liberate them from male sexual tyranny.'[56]

Canada's suffragists definitely tried to play down the physical side of relationships. They constantly exhorted women to become friends and companions to men rather than sexual toys or dolls.[57] They seemed to feel that, since physical strength still played a prominent role in work and in defence, women had to emphasize the spiritual and intellectual side of their nature in order to claim equality. It could be argued that they feared sex because it accentuated physical needs and kept the weaker woman in a subservient relationship. As Alice Chown explained, 'So long as woman accepts indiscriminate sex relations, so long will she be subject to man.'[58]

The claim to represent a higher morality clearly gave the women a position of power and respect in the community. It allowed them to demand the right to become the moral arbiters for the nation and to discipline deviant males. But it also tied them to very traditional virtues. Chastity may have given them a certain control over their person but it also made it difficult for them to assess the advantages of artificial birth control devices, for example. For years these were castigated as one more means of facilitating male licentiousness.[59] Yet, because of the obvious decline in the birth rate in these years, it is clear that many women knew of and were prepared to use artificial contraception.[60] The commitment to sexual restraint in this instance may, therefore, have cut the women suffragists off from the wider female community. This may have been true in yet another way since the decision to reject sexuality as an evil clearly delayed the prospect of female sexual liberation.

The female suffragists managed therefore to raise their status and that of women generally by capitalizing on the anxiety over the deterioration of the race. Housekeeping became a profession. Their role as reformers seemed justified. Their higher morality made them the leaders in the battle against impurity and venereal disease.

More than any other single factor, however, the commitment to race regeneration placed a premium on women's traditional duties and virtues. Women were needed in the home to guarantee the health of the new generation. Their voices were needed in the community primarily to guarantee its morality. Because the female suffragists were equally committed to the proliferation and regeneration of the Anglo-Saxon race, they were quite content to fulfil these roles and did not question the limitations they imposed on women's attitudes and activities.

8

The Suffrage Fringe:
Labour and the Organized Farmer

The organized farmers in the Prairie West – the Saskatchewan and Manitoba Grain Growers' Associations and the United Farmers of Alberta – and some elements of the Canadian labour movement were among the earliest and staunchest advocates of woman suffrage. Yet very few farm or labour men or women managed to penetrate the ranks of the overt suffrage societies which form the basis of this study. These remained predominantly an urban phenomenon, dominated and run by male and female journalists, lawyers, teachers, clerics, and businessmen, a professional and entrepreneurial élite. In general, farmers, their wives, and members of the labouring classes preferred to work for the ballot through their own organizations rather than join the suffragists, who showed little real understanding of their problems. The women in these groups managed to cooperate on occasion with the female suffragists in several joint ventures for specifically female goals: for example, to win equal homesteading privileges and a dower law.[1] But a series of confrontations between the suffragists on the one hand and the farm and labour women on the other suggests that more divided than united them. The ideological and tactical disagreements between the women indicate that the suffragists had difficulty conceiving of women's problems as an issue apart and that in general they reflected the attitudes of the social élite to which they belonged.

I

Labour was one of the earliest supporters of female enfranchisement in Canada. Certain labour newspapers, the *Winnipeg Voice*,
for example, began publishing articles in favour of the measure
as early as 1902, the same year a British Columbia labour conference passed a resolution supporting woman suffrage.[2] But
labour, of course, was not a monolith. Broadly speaking, Canadian labour adopted three different but often interconnected
approaches to reform. The conservative element, the business
unionists, were mainly skilled workers who followed the American Federation of Labor's policies under Samuel Gompers. Long-
term goals were subordinated to short-term gains for skilled
workers under this policy. Business unionists eschewed independent labour politics until 1906 and showed great hostility to
any form of socialism. 'Labourites,' on the other hand, promoted
independent labour politics along the lines of the British Labour
Party. A third small but not insignificant sector in the labour
movement called for the abolition of capitalist exploitation and
the wage system.[3]

The suffrage issue divided the labour movement in spite of
some official support. Business unionists who sided with the
Conservative Party came to support suffrage only at the last
minute. For them, woman suffrage was a means of protecting the
skilled worker's bargaining position against unskilled women
workers. Unorganized and untrained women undercut men's
wages and weakened the union's effectiveness. With political
recognition women might improve their position in the market-
place and make it easier for them to win equal wages. In the
mind of almost every unionist the two reforms of woman suffrage and equal pay were inseparable. In 1916, for example, the
president of the Canadian Trades and Labour Congress, J.C.
Watters, promised Toronto suffragist Constance Hamilton to
support votes for women in exchange for an agreement on the
principle of equal pay.[4] Labourites meanwhile supported woman
suffrage because they believed that if working-class women had
a vote, they stood a better chance of electing working-class
representatives. Like the business unionists, they hoped that

capitalism could be reformed from within. Labour radicals on the other hand who had little confidence in political action or parliament doubted that woman suffrage, a purely parliamentary reform, would achieve anything. In 1915, the *Winnipeg Voice*, begun as an independent labour paper, endorsed the socialist view that the wage system needed to be abolished completely. Therefore, the *Voice* claimed, the woman's vote had limited value because it rested on the belief that the 'present system of wage labour and capital is all right if you give it a little tinkering.' These radicals detected the suffragists' class bias and this made them even more cautious about the movement's usefulness. The *Voice* called the Winnipeg Political Equality League 'a left wing of the Liberal Party,' scorned its members for their patronizing attitude towards working women, and dismissed them as 'noisy advocates' campaigning for a 'pet hobby.'[5] Despite these hesitations, socialists were forced to take up the question and eventually came to support female enfranchisement. Even the Socialist Party of Canada adopted woman suffrage after an initial phase of denouncing all meliorative reforms.

The suffragists' behaviour and attitudes meanwhile gave labour supporters good grounds for their suspicions. True 'paternalists,' the suffragists found it difficult to let labour do things for itself. They opposed strikes and unionization and recommended palliatives like factory legislation to remove the most blatant evils of the industrial system. Constance Hamilton, for example, rejected the idea of unions and argued that the solution to industrial unrest lay simply 'in the shortening of hours of labour.' Emily Murphy believed that the 'machinations of lawyers' (her version of the outside agitator) drove workers to strike, and that most workers were quite capable of self-sacrifice and even of genuine affection for their employers. She added that strikes ought to be avoided at almost any cost because 'they punished the operator far too dearly both in the expenditure of nerve and of money.'[6] Despite their political cautiousness, suffragists courted the support of labour in order to win some powerful new allies and to increase their chances of success. Mrs Hamilton, hardly a labour enthusiast, made the deal with Watters for this reason.

At the same time the suffragists generally ignored female workers since the suffrage movement had neither the organizational base nor the political strength to mobilize them. On one occasion, in 1912, Alice Chown, who was one of Canada's few radical suffragists, tried to elicit support among her fellow Toronto suffragists for the New York ladies' garment workers' strike. She failed. The women reacted favourably only when she had some tale of hardship to tell. They refused, it seems, to support the strike, because they feared that an overt association with such an unpopular cause would jeopardize the whole suffrage campaign.[7] Canadian suffragists, moreover, made little effort to conscript working-class women into their associations. In fact, according to Flora Macdonald Denison, they treated the working women who dared to attend their meetings like social pariahs, belittling them for their poor dress and ungrammatical speech.[8] Only in the more radical political climate of British Columbia did one extraordinary woman, Helena Gutteridge, manage to acquire sufficient political prestige to surmount this social barrier and join a regular suffrage society, the Pioneer Political Equality League. Yet Gutteridge did not see eye to eye with the suffragists. She ranked enfranchisement second in importance to unionization, which she considered the working woman's only *real* defence against exploitation. Gutteridge also criticized the suffragists' stance on protective legislation. Laws restricting women's hours and conditions of labour, in her opinion, only made women less employable. She considered the idea of a minimum wage 'an experiment' male workers wished to try out on women.[9]

The ideological differences between the suffragists and working-class women were dramatically demonstrated in the confrontation between the suffragists and the Women's Labour League. The WLL was a different type of working-class woman's society, composed, originally, of the wives and daughters of trade unionists. Based on a British model founded by Margaret Macdonald, the Labour Leagues were really an extension of the male unions. By 1910 Canada had branches in Port Arthur, Fort William, Winnipeg, and Toronto. The women in the Leagues encouraged working women to form unions primarily to protect their own husbands and fathers from wage undercutters. They realized that their men, and consequently they themselves, would prosper only if women were organized along lines similar to the men. The League leaders endorsed woman suffrage in order to facilitate organization among working women and to win equal pay for equal work.[10]

Although both the Leagues and the suffrage societies agreed on the need for a vote, the relationship between them was strained. Ada Muir, one of the founders of the Winnipeg League, maintained that the suffragists represented one distinct interest group, the professionals, while the Labour Leagues spoke for another, the working men and women of the nation. She considered the suffragists part of a professional monopoly which was trying to take effective control of the country through the reform movement. The large numbers of professionals in the suffrage societies undoubtedly strengthened this suspicion. Mrs Muir argued that the public health, social welfare, and education reform campaigns were simply attempts on the part of professionals (doctors, social workers, teachers) to make their services indispensable to the community and guarantee themselves an income. Because professionals used the state to create conditions conducive to their occupational security, by encouraging the building of more public schools, imposing public health standards, and legislating morality, Mrs Muir and many other members of the working class suspected the state interventionist philosophy.[11]

The prohibition issue created additional tension. Many working-class men and women considered prohibition to be class legislation, designed to impose middle-class standards on them. The suffragists, on the other hand, usually favoured prohibition. For a time, the issue lay dormant. Then in 1918, with prohibition in force, the First World War nearing its end, and industrial unrest at a new high in Canada, the Winnipeg Women's Labour League publicly endorsed the sale of light beer and wine as a deliberate affront to the prohibitionist suffragists.[12] Finally, in the same year, the suffragists revealed their true colours by giving their support to a group of Local Council women who acted as scabs during a Winnipeg strike.[13] In protest, the Labour

League withdrew all support from the Manitoba Political Education League, the successor to the Political Equality League, thus ending the period of toleration and accommodation between the two groups.

A few suffragists actually joined the ranks of labour, which suggests the danger in making facile generalizations about the character of the woman suffrage movement. Although they were a minority, these men and women represented an important ideological tributary to the mainstream. Their attitudes illustrate the way in which a state interventionist philosophy could lead to radical politics. Nonetheless, their radicalism had its limitations. They seem to have had difficulty escaping the paternalistic attitudes which characterized the movement as a whole. Moreover, the goals of social harmony and racial progress which motivated many reformers inhibited their social vision.

In 1915 the District Labour Council of Toronto hired suffragist Laura Hughes to investigate conditions in local plants engaged in the manufacture of war supplies. Miss Hughes obtained an undercover post as a factory worker in the Joseph Simpson Knitting Company. She conducted an on-the-spot inspection and submitted her observations in a report which the District Council sent on to the Minister of Labour. Miss Hughes' experience converted her into an outspoken labour sympathizer. She became a popular lecturer at Toronto Labour Conventions and in 1916 was elected second vice-president of the Greater Toronto Labour Party.[14] Yet despite her apparent radicalism, Miss Hughes failed to break the bond of middle-class morality. Helena Gutteridge considered her little better than a patronizing reformer and repudiated her for appealing to the 'humanity' of the employers and for recommending clubs to 'reform' working girls. She also criticized Miss Hughes for her obsession with political solutions. Laura Hughes promoted a political party of labour, while Helena Gutteridge encouraged unionization and workers' political action without the intermediary of a labour party.[15]

A second Toronto suffragist, Harriet Dunlop Prenter, the president of a small group called simply the Political Equality League, also joined the labour movement. She submitted articles to the Toronto labour paper, the *Industrial Banner*, and lectured on behalf of the Labour Lecture Bureau. In 1920 she became the assistant secretary of the Toronto Independent Labour Party. Her social vision, however, did not differ significantly from that of the majority of suffragists. She endorsed a limited notion of equality and did not challenge class privilege. The means, not the ends, distinguished her from the larger body of suffragists. She discarded 'uplifting' and 'committees,' the traditional strategy of the reformer, in order to co-operate with the 'intelligent efforts' of organized labour.[16]

Rose Henderson, the Montreal suffragist and probation officer, agreed with Mrs Prenter that significant change would come about only if the newly enfranchised women joined forces with labour and marched together 'to attain the emancipation of the toiling masses.' But middle-class assumptions affected her analysis. Mrs Henderson led the campaign for mothers' pensions, which aimed ultimately at removing women from the labour force and returning them to their homes, hardly a viable alternative for most working women.[17]

Tactics sometimes brought suffragists and labour spokesmen together, but in general the suffragists remained suspicious of labour organization. Strikes implied conflict and conflict had no place in their design for society. Nor did the women in the movement take more than a token interest in the problems of working-class women. The suffrage movement was less a 'woman's movement' than an attempt on the part of particular men and women, predominantly urban professionals and entrepreneurs, to supervise society.

II

Tensions also arose between the organized farm women in the Prairies and the Western female suffragists who, as in the East, tended to be mainly urban professionals. As in the case of labour, economic interests prevented sexual cohesion. The organized farm women wanted a vote for several reasons: to rectify certain injustices against women, to strengthen the Protestant, Anglo-Saxon clique to which they belonged, and to increase the political awareness and representation of the agrarian sector. The suffragists could readily sympathize with the first two goals but the last made it difficult for the women to work together.

Developments within the West encouraged the growth of political consciousness among Canada's farming population. It may be true that the entire West felt constrained by the Eastern presence, but the farmers seemed to suffer more, and more vocally. They experienced specific economic grievances which did not equally affect the cities. The farmers, for example, bought in a protected market and sold in an unprotected one. The world wheat price fluctuated outside their control, yet at home the protective tariff compelled them to buy the necessities of life and much of their farm equipment at prices only partially competitive.[18]

Meanwhile, the Western cities began to resemble Eastern urban centres. Urban growth proceeded at a rapid rate in Western Canada, the urban segment of the population having risen, in Alberta, from 25.4 per cent in 1901 to 36.8 per cent in 1911 and in Manitoba, from 27.6 per cent to 43.4 per cent.[19] The culture of the city alarmed the farmer. 'Hotbeds of vice' and centres of 'alien congestion,' cities represented the opposite of what they thought to be their virtuous prairie farm life. Finally, the farmers began to fear the disproportionate political influence of the urban sector, particularly of the professional and entrepreneurial élite who ruled the cities. To protect their special interests and strengthen their political voice, the farmers decided to organize, forming the Territorial Grain Growers' Association in 1902, the Manitoba Grain Growers' Association in 1903, the United Farmers of Alberta in 1909. Later in the century they turned to independent political action (the Progressive Party) to redress the balance in favour of the country.[20]

The growing political consciousness of the farmers encouraged them to involve their women in an attempt to mobilize their entire strength. They urged their wives and daughters to join their organizations and to form co-ordinate auxiliaries. Logically, they concluded that in order for rural women to help implement the farmers' programme they needed a political voice. The Saskatchewan Grain Growers' Association and the United Farmers of Alberta both passed resolutions in favour of

woman suffrage in 1913, a few years before the organized suffrage campaign really got under way in the West.[21] Moreover, like
the urban reformers, many rural leaders conceived of good,
Christian women as the 'harbingers of civilization' and wished
to enlist their assistance in taming the West and controlling
urban vice, principally drunkenness and prostitution.[22] Western
farm women eagerly joined the new associations, demonstrating
an untapped political consciousness and a keen desire to organize. A referendum report issued by the *Grain Growers' Guide* in
1914 confirmed that farm women were as aware as their men of
the needs of the agricultural community. The *Guide* asked its
readers their opinions on the major political questions of the
day, which included the entire farmers' platform: direct democracy, free trade, the single tax, and government ownership of
public utilities. The women endorsed reform in the same high
proportions as the men.[23]

The political awareness of the farm women produced a conflict of interest between them and the urban professional women
in the suffrage societies. The history of the formation of the farm
women's associations and the Prairie suffrage societies confirms
that Western women divided sharply along urban-rural lines.
When the Saskatchewan Grain Growers decided in 1913 to inau-
gurate a female auxiliary, the secretary, F.W. Green, invited
suffragist Francis Marion Beynon to help. She did so by publiciz-
ing the meeting through her column in the *Grain Growers' Guide*.
Several other suffragists, notably Nellie McClung, Lillian Beynon Thomas, and Cora Hind, attended the opening meeting.[24] In
Alberta, Jean Reed, a former British suffragist and a journalist,
became the first president of the Woman's Auxiliary to the
United Farmers of Alberta (UFA).[25] But once the organizations
were under way, the wives and daughters of farmers took over
the executive positions and the suffragists retreated to their city-
based societies. Violet Jackson MacNaughton, an English-born
schoolteacher who arrived in Saskatchewan in 1909 and a year
later married local farmer John MacNaughton, became the first
Women's Grain Growers' Association (WGGA) president. In 1915
Jean Reed retired in favour of a local farmer's wife, Irene Parlby,
whose father, Colonel Marryat, had been one of the main insti-

gators behind the formation of the Alix local of the UFA, and whose husband, Walter Parlby, became its first president. The suffragists continued to comment favourably on the new farm women's organizations but they no longer joined actively in the proceedings – the auxiliaries now belonged to the farm women.

Meanwhile, the Western suffrage societies, like those in the East, were strictly an urban phenomenon, directed by professional men and women or the wives of professionals and businessmen. The Manitoba Political Equality League (PEL) was ruled by a city executive and operated out of Winnipeg and not the surrounding countryside.[26] Alberta never acquired a provincial suffrage body, but in 1915 two local suffrage societies emerged in the two largest urban centres, Calgary and Edmonton. Only in Saskatchewan did farm women initiate the suffrage campaign. In 1913, Premier Walter Scott received over 170 letters and 190 petitions containing 2,500 names, all from country women, again attesting to the farm women's political awareness.[27] This unusual situation disturbed Violet MacNaughton, who felt that, unless city women became equally vociferous, the movement could hardly claim a broad national base.[28] In an attempt to stir the city women out of the lethargy, she organized the Saskatchewan Political Equal Franchise Board (PEFB) in 1915 to co-ordinate the efforts of the WGGA, the Woman's Christian Temperance Union (WCTU), and the few small city societies which already existed. Mrs MacNaughton apparently underestimated the strength of the city leagues, however, for they dominated the first PEFB meeting and introduced a method of selecting representatives which guaranteed their ascendancy at future meetings. Each city franchise league received one representative for every twenty-five members, while the WGGA and the WCTU received a restricted total representation of two members each. Representatives from the newly formed suffrage societies in Regina, Moose Jaw, Prince Albert, Yorkton, and Moosemin, all growing town communities, took over the PEFB executive, reaffirming the traditional pattern of the urban-based suffrage association.[29]

Mrs MacNaughton had anticipated that city and farm women might have difficulty working together and for this reason had suggested that the Franchise Board act simply as a clearing house for ideas, along the same lines as the National Council of Women of Canada (NCWC). But soon the Board completely ignored its founder and her advice and introduced a single platform for both city and country women.[30] The programme repelled Mrs MacNaughton for two reasons. First, the Board showed too great a willingness to co-operate with Eastern suffragists. Mrs MacNaughton, a good barometer of farm sentiment, distrusted the East and its representatives.[31] Second, Mrs MacNaughton objected to the suffragists' obvious Liberal bias. Personally she favoured the formation of an independent farmers' party. Alienated by these developments, the farm women declared that they no longer considered the Board representative of farm women's interests and in 1916 refused to endorse it. Except for the two token representatives who occasionally attended meetings, the Franchise Board now rested completely in the hands of city women.

The reason for the dichotomy between the suffragists and the farm women was simply that economic interests separated them. Granted, country and city women faced many common problems – the drudgery of the domestic routine and unjust property and marriage laws. But the women interpreted the causes of their problems, especially their economic problems, differently. The suffragists attributed the farm women's hardships to their husbands. Francis Beynon, for example, blamed the farmers for refusing to purchase the new kitchen conveniences to lighten their wives' work load.[32] Vocal leaders among the farm women stressed that their husbands were not at fault. According to Irene Parlby, tariffs, not men, were the villains and the real reason why farm women were overworked or grew old before their time. Tariffs raised the price of farm machinery and left little surplus income for luxuries such as household labour-saving devices.[33] The organized farm women, therefore, placed economic above sexual discrimination. They felt no more oppressed than their husbands, with whom they faced a common oppressor, the Eastern interests. They wanted a vote to help protect women against the visible inequities of the system but, more than this, to help their men recast the economic structure in favour of the agrarian sector. In Mrs Parlby's words, 'First and foremost as organized farm women we stand shoulder to shoulder with the men's organization in the demand for a reconstruction of our economic system.'[34]

The divergent attitudes of the farm women and the suffragists surfaced in their quarrel over the Homemakers' Clubs and the Women's Institutes, government-sponsored organizations designed to upgrade the farm wife's domestic capabilities. The Women's Institutes were founded in Ontario in 1898 by Adelaide Hoodless at the suggestion of G.C. Creelman, the Superintendent of the Farmers' Institutes, and soon became popular throughout Manitoba and Alberta. In Saskatchewan, the Agricultural College Department of the Saskatchewan government launched a parallel association, the Homemakers' Clubs. Both groups had the same purpose, to improve the quality of homemaking among farm women by offering them instruction in cooking, sewing, health, and hygiene. Both also received financial assistance from their respective provincial governments. The Institutes received a grant of ten dollars a year to assist them in holding their meetings and had access to the Department of Education travelling libraries and to literature from the Department of Agriculture.[35] Similarly, the Homemakers became a ward of the Saskatchewan government and received a stipend of three dollars yearly, which the government claimed gave it the right to 'supervise and govern their activity.'[36] The governments considered it a worthwhile investment to raise 'the general standard of health and morals of the people' and thereby contribute to the emergence of a powerful nation.[37]

As reformers, the suffragists were dedicated to improving the health and excellence of the race, and they therefore enthusiastically promoted the new associations. They considered them the rural counterpart of the urban domestic science courses that most suffrage societies endorsed. Several suffragists assumed prominent positions in the new societies. Emily Murphy and Nellie McClung became department heads in the Institutes while Lillian Beynon Thomas organized and directed the Homemakers' Clubs.[38]

Meanwhile the organized farm women were suspicious of the new associations. They believed that the Liberal governments in

Saskatchewan and Alberta feared the potential power of the organized farmers' movement and introduced these conservative women's societies to draw attention away from the WGGA and the UFWA. In the 1890s the Patrons of Industry in Ontario had accused Queen's Park of creating the Farmers' Institutes for a similar reason, to channel and quell rural discontent.[39] Violet MacNaughton called the Homemakers' Clubs 'an appendage of the Provincial Liberal Party,' designed to compete with and to help suppress the politically dangerous farm women's associations.[40] Irene Parlby considered the Alberta Institute nothing but 'another political machine,' bought and paid for by the government.[41] The provincial Liberal Parties, despite their connection with the Prairie reform movement, had not quite convinced farmers or farm women that they represented their interests. It was becoming increasingly clear that nothing but an independent farmers' party could speak for farmers.

The Western suffragists and the organized farm women, therefore, while united in their desire for a ballot, were divided by party and economic interests. Within an emerging Western consciousness country and city vied for political influence. The suffragists lined up with the reform-minded Liberals, the farm women with the organized farmers. The suffragists represented an urban professional and entrepreneurial élite; the farm women, a group of primary producers.

III

The organized farm women had disagreements with Eastern as well as with Western suffragists, and for basically the same reason, the incompatibility of agrarian and urban professional values. In 1918, Constance Hamilton and several other Toronto suffragists from the breakaway 'national' association, the National Equal Franchise Union, established a Woman's Party, ostensibly to continue pursuing the elusive goal of sexual equality, following the granting of the vote to women.[42] The Woman's Party, dominated by the East, attracted little support in either the urban or rural West, but Violet MacNaughton and Irene Parlby, representing the farm element, became its most vociferous critics.

They attacked three planks in the party's platform – war till victory, stronger Imperial ties, and opposition to labour unionization – their views on which illustrate the different priorities of the agricultural West and the business-oriented East.

The WGGA and the UFWA exhibited a greater tolerance towards Germany after the war than did the Eastern suffragists. Irene Parlby denounced the Woman's Party's pledge 'not to buy, sell, or use any articles made in Germany or by her allies,' to withdraw all subject populations from Germany's jurisdiction, and to reduce Germany's mineral resources. She predicted that such behaviour simply guaranteed the antagonism which would produce another war at some time in the future.[43] Some important farm women had definite pacifist sympathies. During the war, for example, Violet MacNaughton corresponded with Laura Hughes, the head of the Toronto branch of the Women's International League for Peace and Freedom, and continued a campaign for peace into the 1920s.[44]

The WGGA and the UFWA both rejected the appeal for close Imperial ties. The Woman's Party recommended that the 'natural resources, the essential industries, and the transport system of the Empire be under strictly Imperial ownership and control.' The economic implications of this plan disturbed farm women. They believed that the position of the farmer in Canada was unique, that even the federal government stood too far removed to understand his problems, and that, therefore, no remote Imperial body could possibly hope to grasp his needs.[45]

Although various attempts at farm-labour coalitions failed dismally during this period, the organized farm women spoke of themselves as members of a larger producing class which included labour. They described farmers and labourers as 'brothers beneath the skin.' For this reason they could not condone the Woman's Party's patronizing attitude towards labour and its general anti-union stance, which Parlby called a 'knock-out blow' to democratic principle.[46] They defiantly suggested that, despite its claim to speak for all of Canadian womanhood, the Woman's Party represented only the Eastern ladies of wealth and leisure, the plutocracy, and indirectly, Eastern vested interests.

Beyond the platform, the farm women objected to the whole idea of a *woman's* party, one founded on sex distinctions. They believed that economics, not the 'antediluvian fetish of sex distinction and discrimination,' moved people.[47] Some women, they argued, believed in free trade and others believed in protection, depending on their class. According to the journalist Mary McCallum, women, like men, fell into their respective occupational groups: 'The women labour class became a part of the labour party as a whole; farm women had a voice in the platform of agriculture.' It was foolish, she maintained, ever to expect women as a group to unite on a national policy.[48] On the other hand, the president of the Woman's Party, Constance Hamilton, argued that women constituted a 'class' unto themselves and that they were quite justified in forming a party. 'If it is of advantage to agriculturalists to unite for their own special interests, then it is equally advantageous to unite women for their own special interests,' she declared.[49] Under the heading 'Special Women's Interests,' the party listed the reforms which women had fought for during the past four decades, reforms most women agreed upon: equal pay for equal work, equal marriage laws including equal conditions of divorce, equality of parental rights, raising the age of consent, and equal homesteading privileges.[50] Mrs Hamilton either failed to realize that parts of the party's platform, particularly those dealing with national economic policy, offended certain women in the community, or she did not consider their opinions of any importance. The call for closer Imperial supervision of the economy and the opposition to labour unions demonstrate that Mrs Hamilton represented an urban social élite and not all women, as she would have liked to believe. Irene Parlby realized this. In her opinion, the category 'Special Women's Interests' simply provided a 'sugar-coating' to the bitter pill of unsound economic policy which ran throughout the whole programme.[51] Labour women also recognized the bias of the Woman's Party. The editor of the Woman's Page in the *Industrial Banner* labelled it an 'annex' to the Conservative Party.[52]

Despite many common objectives, therefore, women at the turn of the century had closer ties to their own particular social class than to each other. In part, they were caught up in the heightened occupational consciousness of the era,[53] evident in the proliferation of businessmen's associations, professional societies, labour unions, and farm co-operatives. In part they demonstrated the political truth that economic considerations dominate ideology.

The suffragists may have claimed to represent all women, but much of their policy clearly appealed only to urban professionals and entrepreneurs. Politically they supported the parties which represented these groups, which left farm and labour women to find their own spokesmen. After enfranchisement, predictably, women followed voting patterns determined by their political and economic affiliations.

9

The Politics of Success

In any society the tactics of a privileged order are always the same tactics. Declare in the first place that the demand is impossible; insist when it has been proved to be possible that the time for its translation into statute has not yet come; then when it is clear that there seems to be an urgency about it, that the time is coming but that this is not yet the time; then when an angry clamour surrounds the demand, insist that you cannot yield to violence; and when finally you are driven to yield say that it is because you have been intellectually convinced that the perspective of events has changed.[1]

The takeover of the suffrage movement by social reformers committed to other causes guaranteed its success. The general reform movement became very powerful in early-twentieth-century Canada as its analysis of social problems seemed increasingly relevant. The suffragists profited politically from the strength of their allies. Moreover, once it became clear that female enfranchisement was imminent, politicians from all shades of the political spectrum proved willing to introduce the legislation on the off-chance that the women might feel some sense of obligation to support their benefactors.

Ideologically, the domination of the movement by men and women who had no intention of upsetting the traditional familial order, and who defended votes for women on the grounds that women's morality, religiosity, and piety were needed in society, took away any sting the issue might once have had. The feminist cry for women's equal educational and occupational rights became muted and died. Once legislators became convinced that woman suffrage meant a strengthening rather than a questioning of social norms, women had not long to wait for a ballot.

I

The first federal support for woman suffrage came from an unexpected source and suggests that, even very early in the piece, some legislators were aware that the reform could have moderating, even conservative effects. In 1883 John A. Macdonald attached an appeal for the federal enfranchisement of propertied widows and spinsters to his Franchise Bill. Suffrage activity in Canada had only just begun and not a single suffrage petition had yet reached the Parliament. Macdonald seemed to be running well ahead of public opinion, an unusual posture for a Conservative Prime Minister.

The question of property, it seems, was all important. Conservative politics rested on the premise that property required representation, and Macdonald was simply being true to this creed by suggesting that it apply equally to women.[2] Only widows and spinsters who held property in their own right were to join the electorate in Macdonald's scheme. No doubt he believed that they, like the propertied men in the community, would help keep him in power. Macdonald feared the influence of the newly enfranchised working class and simply wished to compensate by tapping a new reservoir of Conservative support. At one stage he even suggested giving propertied *married* women a vote since that would double the number of propertied voters in the community, again with predictable conservative results. Macdonald also realized that most women were socially 'preservative' and that he could therefore count on them to 'strengthen the defences against the eruption of an unbridled democracy.'[3] He anticipated no serious role change for women, not even their election to the legislature.[4] He simply wanted to give a second voice to the home and to garner more Conservative votes.

Those opposed to the reform raised the spectre of the liberated female abandoning her family to lodge a vote. To use the words of one Member of Parliament: 'I believe rather in domestic economy than in political economy for females. That is their domain ...'[5] Another waxed poetical about how politics would corrupt the female character, turning the docile, long-suffering female into an Amazon:

> She matches meekness with his might
>   And patience with his power to act –
> His judgement with her quicker sight,
>   And wins by subtlety and tact
> The battles he can only fight.
>
> And she who strives to take the van
>   In conflict, or the common way,
> Does outrage to the heavenly plan,
>   And outrage to the finer clay
> That makes her beautiful to man.[6]

In retrospect, Macdonald was quite correct and his opponents had little to fear; woman suffrage produced no radical role reversal or personality transformation in women.

As early as 1883, therefore, some Canadian politicians recognized women's potential usefulness as defenders of the status quo. As the nineteenth century advanced, and as more challenges to the traditional social structure were thrown up, more and more men and women came around to Macdonald's point of view. This argument eventually won women the vote.

The history of Macdonald's Franchise Bill forecast the future of the suffrage movement in another way, for it demonstrated that the actual granting of votes to women would become more a political than an ideological battle. It is difficult to judge the sincerity of Macdonald's commitment to woman suffrage, but the evidence suggests that he was a genuine convert. In public statements and private correspondence he never once renounced his stand.[7] But Macdonald was still first and foremost the politician and he soon found out that neither the majority in his party nor the majority in the House supported his position. Following this discovery, according to contemporary reports, Macdonald and his party reached an agreement about the fate of the Act. One political commentator accused Sir John of promising his supporters in caucus that the woman's clause would be thrown over to satisfy Quebec, the most vigorous opponent of votes for women.[8] Another suggested that Sir John personally put up one of his own supporters from Nova Scotia to move the amendment *excluding* women from the operation of the Act.[9]

If any of this were true, what could Macdonald have hoped to gain from introducing the measure in the first place? One thing is certain – the real issue was not woman suffrage. The new Franchise Act touched another, more sensitive nerve. It proposed giving the federal government the power to appoint revising officers for electoral lists, thereby removing them from the jurisdiction of the provincial county councils. The Act then divided Liberals and Conservatives on the traditional issue of provincial versus federal rights. It is possible that Macdonald left the woman's clause in the bill 'as a buffer,' to allow the Opposition to expend their force on a minor point and to draw fire from the 'real gist' of the bill, the appointment of revising officers.

And what of the Liberals? Most of the debate in *favour* of the clause came from the *Opposition* side of the House. The Liberals probably suspected Macdonald's tactics and hoped to see them backfire, further adding to his embarrassment by helping the bill pass despite the opposition of his own party. The lengthy debate was, in fact, a Liberal tactic, designed to protract and defeat and perhaps to get a favourable compromise on the section giving the government power to appoint electoral revisors. The debate lasted twenty-six hours, as members recited every traditional argument for and against woman suffrage. In the end, very few proved genuine devotees. The amendment to strike out the provision giving the vote to women finally carried, seventy-eight in favour to fifty-one opposed.[10]

II

In the new century politics played a crucial role in the suffrage battle.[11] While it might seem that ideologically all Liberals ought to have endorsed woman suffrage and all Conservatives to have opposed it, this did not happen in the political arena. Parties added woman suffrage to their rostrum only when it seemed to their political advantage to do so.

In the Prairies, the first provinces to enfranchise Canadian women, a reform coalition composed of temperance men and organized farmers pressed for woman suffrage because they believed it would advance their particular goals. In Manitoba, the reformers fought a long and hard battle against Sir Rodmond Roblin, the Conservative Premier and the friend of business and liquor interests.[12] The Liberal Party, under T.C. Norris, became the party of reform and endorsed woman suffrage along with prohibition, direct legislation, civil service reform, workmen's compensation, mothers' allowances, and child welfare legislation. In 1916 the Liberals came to power and stood by their electoral promises, making Manitoba the first province to enfranchise women. In Alberta and Saskatchewan the suffrage movement took a fairly easy road owing to the persistence of the farmers' organizations and other progressive groups which had made woman suffrage part of their reform package. The Liberal Premiers, Sifton and Scott respectively, soon followed the Manitoba example and gave women the vote in 1916.[13]

This granting of votes to women in three provinces forced the issue of federal enfranchisement on Ottawa, since, according to the 1898 franchise law, federal electoral lists were drawn from provincial lists. In 1916 William Pugsley, the former New Brunswick Premier and a long-standing defender of women's political rights, moved that the Federal Parliament grant voting privileges to women who already possessed a provincial franchise.[14] The Prime Minister, Robert Borden, was unsure where he stood constitutionally and appealed for advice to his shrewd political lieutenant, Arthur Meighen.

The political situation determined Meighen's response. The Conservatives were about to force an election and were going to stand on the issue of compulsory conscription for overseas war service. Meighen already feared the number of alien voters in the Prairies and did not want this number enlarged by adding female aliens to the electoral lists. The large French representation, traditionally Liberal and suspect because of its reluctant war contribution, increased in Meighen's eyes the chance of a

Conservative defeat.[15] Futhermore, he felt that foreign and French women would be far more likely to exercise their ballot than English women, who, in his opinion, took no interest in politics.[16] For these reasons Meighen recommended that for the time being Borden take the ground that 'in so radical an alteration of the whole basis of the franchise there should be no discrimination between the Provinces.'[17] In normal circumstances, Meighen went on to explain, he would recommend leaving this to the provinces, but, owing to the absence of soldiers overseas, foreigners controlled many constituencies and made the possibility of a pro-war, pro-conscription victory unlikely.

In 1917 Ontario followed the Prairie lead and gave its women a provincial ballot. For years the women had petitioned both parties asking that woman suffrage be added to their platforms. The Liberals, led by the prohibitionist Newton Rowell, finally relented shortly before the 1917 session opened. But the Conservatives held power, and the Conservative Party, first under J.P. Whitney and after 1914 under William Hearst, had consistently rejected the women's request. Then, in 1917, a Conservative, J.W. Johnson, tabled two bills which provided for full municipal and provincial female voting privileges.[18] Hearst performed an admirable volte-face and now defended the women's right to vote on the basis of their performance during the war. One historian has suggested that Borden exerted pressure on Hearst to pass this legislation because, in anticipation of his own franchise bill, he thought it wise to make Ontario women beholden to the Conservative Party, to offset the Liberal power in the Prairies.[19] Whether or not this is true, Hearst, like most politicians at the time, realized that the reform could not be resisted long and that he might as well take the opportunity to feather the Conservative Party's political nest with thankful female voters.

In British Columbia, under Premiers McBride and Bowser, the Conservatives had remained in power from 1903 to 1916. The Liberals, under Brewster, had backed woman suffrage for years. Bowser decided to divorce the suffrage question from party politics by making it the subject of a referendum, to be held at the same time as the 1916 election.[20] The male electorate agreed by a vote of two to one that women should have the right to vote.[21] The referendum failed Bowser's purpose, however, for it aroused the hostility of the suffrage groups who felt that the referendum was simply a device to delay the legislation. Disgusted by this tactic, they compaigned actively for the Liberals, who came to power in 1916 and a year later brought down the suffrage legislation won by the referendum.

With Ontario and British Columbia women now enfranchised, Borden again sought Meighen's advice on the federal status of women who could vote provincially. This time Meighen recommended a Dominion Act along the lines of the recent Saskatchewan and Alberta Acts which denied the vote to aliens. But he added a new stipulation to the proposed federal legislation, giving the nearest female relatives of enlisted men a vote.[22] The question remains why Meighen did not consider granting the vote to all qualified women. He could then have simply disfranchised the female alien in the same way he disfranchised the male. Even Borden, while he agreed that neither men nor women of enemy nationality should vote, failed to see the justice of denying the franchise to good British and Canadian women whose husbands failed to make it overseas because of some physical disability or because of their employment in essential war industries like munitions, mining, and agriculture.[23] Meighen, it seems, continued to fear the votes of the wives of French-Canadian or for that matter English-Canadian slackers. Enfranchising the wives, mothers, and sisters of soldiers practically guaranteed that they would favour conscription. In any event, despite Borden's misgivings, the franchise act followed Meighen's recommendations to the letter and opened the Tories to charges of partisanship and electoral manipulation.

The suffragists displayed mixed feelings toward the Elections Act. Symptomatic of the increased nativism in the country at large, very few objected to the clauses disfranchising enemy aliens. The Beynon sisters called the Act undemocratic on these grounds: 'the organized women of the province will not agree for the women of the province to be divided into two camps – one half voting because of an accident of birth place and the other half barred for the same reason.'[24] The real controversy arose over the question of partial female enfranchisement. The suffragists divided on this issue in much the same manner as they had over the question of pursuing the vote during wartime. The resolute suffragists rejected the Act as a half measure; the more pliant bent to the Government's will. Predictably the CSA condemned the Act as a 'win-the-election' device, designed simply to ensure a pro-conscription Conservative majority.[25] The NEFU, composed of social reform suffragists who had a prior commitment to the country's strength and survival, eagerly endorsed the Act as a 'win-the-war' measure. In fact, the NEFU had anticipated the problem and had suggested as early as 1915 that an absent soldier be allowed to appoint a wife, mother, or sister as proxy.[26] Nellie McClung, another social reform suffragist, who had one son overseas, pushed the alien argument even further than the government legislation. In 1916 she asked Borden to give only British-born women the vote to offset the lower moral tone of the electorate caused by 'the going away of so many of our best and most public-spirited men.'[27]

Other social reform suffragists played an even more active role in bringing in the Elections Act. Constance Hamilton participated in a partisan, political venture along with the country's leading women reformers, Mrs F.H. Torrington, President of the NCW, Mrs E.A. Stevens, President of the WCTU, and Mrs Albert Gooderham, President of the Imperial Order of the Daughters of Empire (IODE), to test the effect full female enfranchisement might have on the election. These four women, at the Prime Minister's request,[28] sent a telegram to women across Canada asking, 'Would the granting of the Federal franchise to women make conscription assured at the general election, if such is inevitable, taking carefully into consideration the vote of foreign women?' The telegram added the furtive note, 'Please glean your information as quietly as possible.'[29] The straw vote indicated the dangers in full enfranchisement. Violet MacNaughton, for example, warned that in Saskatchewan the language controversy over compulsory English in elementary grades had consolidated the foreign element.[30] These findings probably reinforced Borden's decision to limit female enfranchisement to reliably patriotic women. In 1917 the four women who had conducted the survey issued a public letter, formally approving the Wartime

Elections Act and declaring that Canadian women were willing to forego the privilege of voting in order that Canada 'remain true to her sacred trust to the Canadian men now fighting the battle for freedom.'[31] Not all Canadian women were equally enthusiastic. Indeed the letter attracted a flurry of protests from members of the associations supposedly represented, the NCW, the IODE, and the WCTU, denying that they had been consulted. In the end Mrs Torrington had to print a retraction stating that she spoke only for herself and not for the NCW or for its executive.[32]

While many suffragists claimed to be above party politics, politics still divided them. Several accused the four women of supporting the Act for partisan political reasons; all four possessed husbands who were active Conservatives.[33] On the Prairies where the Liberals had given women the provincial vote, many suffragists retained Liberal sympathies and condemned the Act for its pro-Conservative bias. The Manitoba Political Equality League and the Saskatchewan PEFB both recorded their absolute opposition to a limited franchise for women.[34] The Act also divided the Montreal Suffrage Association along party lines. The majority condemned the legislation and forced the resignation of two important Conservative members, Mr Lansing Lewis and Mrs John Scott.[35] The announcement of Union Government, which ostensibly at least placed the Act above politics and made it strictly a 'win-the-war' measure, ended most protests.[36] Furthermore, Borden's promise that full female enfranchisement would follow within a year convinced the majority of Canadian suffragists to resign themselves to partial but temporary disfranchisement.

In 1918, the year succeeding the Wartime Elections Act, the Borden Government followed through on its promise to extend the federal suffrage to all women of British or Canadian citizenship over twenty-one years of age. Following federal enfranchisement, the political leaders in the remaining provinces realized that it was just a matter of time before women could vote in their provinces also. As a result, in Nova Scotia, New Brunswick, Prince Edward Island, and Newfoundland, the parties competed to see who could enfranchise women first. Quebec women, because of the political and religious situation there, did not obtain a provincial franchise until 1940.[37]

III

Ironically, Canadian women won the suffrage battle when they were least potent. The war detracted from suffrage activity in several ways. It divided the movement, accentuated pre-war differences, and proliferated worthy causes for women volunteers. After 1914, for example, the Montreal Suffrage Association spent no more money on public speakers and assisted instead in patriotic ventures like the Khaki League, the Patriotic Fund, the Soldiers' Wives' League, and the Women's War Register.[38] A Manitoba suffragist complained that, since the outbreak of war, 'it had been impossible to get a meeting together.'[39] Those who continued the campaign, notably the CSA, were berated by female patriots for doing so.

Traditionally, it has been argued that women's patriotic service during the war convinced reluctant males that women were ready for equality. According to the politicians, this was definitely the case. Canadian Premiers and MPs from coast to coast copied British statesmen and sang women's praises for their untiring contribution to the war effort in the factories and in patriotic societies. Invoking the Victorian motto that 'justice comes to those who earn it,' they declared that women had proved that they deserved the country's highest honour, a political vote. Even the die-hard Conservative Premier of Ontario, William Hearst, claimed that the 'splendid part' the women had played in the war had converted him to the cause. He eulogized women for their 'capacity for organization' and their work which unquestioningly proved that they possessed the 'qualification to assist' and the 'ability to advise in the work of the nation.'[40]

The war did prove a turning-point for the suffrage movement, but not for the pious explanation given. Political considerations, many of them a direct result of the war, seem to have been the prime motivation. In the provinces the war accentuated and popularized reform causes, particularly prohibition, and brought to power reform administrations committed to woman suffrage and the rest of the reform programme. The fact that provincial electoral lists were used federally forced the issue upon the central government. Expediency intervened once again. The first instalment of the woman's federal franchise was neither won nor conceded but was imposed to assure the re-election of the pro-conscription Borden Government. No doubt, the eagerness with which the majority of the suffragists embraced the war, willingly subsuming their own campaign, reassured apprehensive politicians that voting women posed no threat. The small feminist clique had been successfully overthrown and the new suffragists evinced fine, patriotic, nativistic feelings and a proper respect for authority and tradition. The taming of the suffrage movement guaranteed its victory.

At base, political pragmatism, not merit, decided the issue. As early as 1885, the debate on the Macdonald Franchise Act showed that few political figures felt a profound ideological aversion to women voting. They awaited, it seems, only the appropriate moment. At first, Canadian politicians defended the position that Canadian women did not want the vote and that, if the suffragists could demonstrate the contrary, they would most certainly receive it. Petitions flooded in. At the same time the international situation, which yearly added to the growing list of states and countries where women could vote, convinced many that woman suffrage was inevitable. The British suffragettes added a note of urgency, for British politicians especially, but also for Canadians who had no desire to see their own women rise up against them. Those with foresight realized it was futile to resist longer. The war gave them the opportunity to appear magnanimous, simultaneously supplying them with a rationalization for their change of heart.

Conclusion

Some eight years after women received the vote, a former Manitoba suffragist, Anne Anderson Perry, analysed its effects. The franchise, she felt, had changed very little. Few women participated in politics, as workers or candidates. Most followed or deferred to men much as they had before. Women, of course, attended political conventions, decorated platforms, and helped male politicians achieve victory, but they continued to take a secondary place to men. There were certainly exceptions, women whose able contribution to public life made conspicuous the absence of larger numbers. Moreover, women seemed indifferent to the great issues which had preoccupied their pre-war interests – child welfare, industrial distress, social and moral reform. Female enfranchisement, she concluded, had simply doubled the electorate and had made no noticeable difference in its character.[1]

Nor did the vote effect a revolution in woman's social status. It added nothing to the 'victories' of the nineteenth century – the release from confining garments, the freedom to appear intelligent, the right of the single woman to work. The social order accommodated only inevitable change or modifications which in no way threatened its existence. The Victorian 'frail vessel' lost precedence to the physically fit, sensibly clothed woman mainly because of the discoveries of eugenics and the desire to evolve a perfect race. Higher education for women promised to develop a woman's 'mental discipline' and subsequently to prepare her to be a better wife and mother. Single women could work simply because economics demanded it: industrialism required a large, cheap work force and population statistics indicated that not every woman would be able to find a husband to support her.

After 1920 female employment figures continued to rise, even female professional employment, but the trend begun in the nineteenth century continued – women filled the lower paid, less prestigious occupations. The categories 'teacher,' 'nurse,' and 'office worker in professional service' made up a high proportion of female professionals while the numbers of female doctors and lawyers remained relatively static.[2] Women involved in manufacturing consistently received lower wages for the same work.[3] The percentage of married women in the labour force increased steadily,[4] a result largely of the pressures of a rising cost of living. Ideologically, however, married women were still not supposed to work. The family remained the basic unit in the social structure and woman's primary function continued to be that of homemaker and child-bearer. As in the case of the single working woman, acceptance would come after the fact, if at all.

In answer to the demand for a more intelligent, better disciplined womanhood, female college enrolment peaked in the 1920s, but afterwards the figures level off.[5] At the graduate level, 1930 recorded the highest female enrolment, 27.9 per cent. By 1958 this had declined to only 16.9 per cent. In 1930 women received 30 per cent of the BAs granted, 20.8 per cent of the MAs, and 11.5 per cent of the PHDs. By 1958 these percentages had been reduced to 23.6, 19.4, and 9.2 per cent respectively.[6]

Facts like these are usually set out as evidence of the failure of the suffrage movement. Before 'failure' can be declared, however, it is imperative to understand the movement's goals and motives. True, the movement may not have succeeded in seriously altering the opportunities available to women, but was this its purpose? People who believe so have been distracted by the voices of a few more militant feminists who proclaimed the battle for a ballot the first of a series of struggles for complete female equality. These women were always a minority, however, and it is inaccurate to impose their expectations upon the movement as a whole. The breakdown of the movement in this book shows that in fact the majority in the suffrage societies were men and women who had no desire to restructure sex roles.

Canada's first suffragists or at least those who *established* the first suffrage societies can legitimately be called feminists on the basis of their programme. Women like Emily Stowe demanded complete equality of the sexes, including equal educational and occupational opportunities. These women were often the first to try to enter male-dominated professions and they were not afraid therefore to challenge convention and risk notoriety. But their message clearly had little appeal to the public at large. They were labelled 'women rightists' and the early societies either stagnated or disbanded after a few years.[7] A few feminists persisted into the twentieth-century societies but they too remained a distinct minority. The occasional voice challenged the supposed blessings of wifehood and motherhood, and demanded that labour and education be sexless. But this was indeed a voice in the wilderness. The tide of public opinion was actually shifting in the completely opposite direction.

Men and women with motives very different from those of this small feminist clique took over the suffrage movement and altered its design and purpose. Their other interests and activities show that they came from a larger reform movement. Some were temperance supporters; others were clerics or good Christian women inspired by the social gospel; many belonged to progressive civic reform groups. Despite its divisions, the larger movement shared certain principles. Chiefly it was inspired by the dramatic social changes which accompanied industrialization and urbanization. By the turn of the century Canada had begun to display all the side-effects of industrial growth – urban concentration, slums, crime, immorality, intemperance, and secularization. These changes distressed certain members of the social élite, mainly the professionals, who had a vision of a march ever onwards to social perfectibility. They therefore took it upon themselves, as the most likely leaders, to introduce reforms to reinstate a sense of order in the chaos.

In order to make Canada into the 'City upon a Hill,' the reformers hoped to reduce crime and delinquency, drinking and prostitution, and signs of social division. They also hoped to create a new and perfect race to people the new land. Much of their programme was 'social-imperialist' in design, aimed at improving the general health and fitness of the population. Their perfect race was to be a homogeneous one, predominantly Anglo-Saxon; immigrants would be converted and assimilated. Woman suffrage attracted the support of many reformers because they believed that it would speed up the implementation of their larger programme. Moreover, female reformers who believed themselves to be members of the ruling meritocracy saw no reason why they should be denied a political voice. The men agreed, especially as the women who now asked for a vote typified the very virtues and values they wished to see enshrined in society – purity and sobriety.

These people flooded into the suffrage societies and took over the leadership of the movement. The reasons they offered for giving women a vote were very different from those used by the feminists. Essentially woman suffrage suggested a simple means of strengthening the stable part of the population. Women were considered to be religious, pure, the 'harbingers of civilization' and the protectors of the home. Their help in controlling social deviants would be welcome. Moreover, the reformers wanted to strengthen the family, which they considered the foundation of their new social order, and believed that woman suffrage would double its representation. For these reasons women were invited into the 'public sphere,' but only in a very limited capacity. The vote meant simply a public voice for their domestic virtues.

In the reformers' hands, woman suffrage lost all identification with the feminist call to enter and compete in the male domain. Since their new social order depended upon the proper training and nurturing of the next generation, emphasis was placed on the importance of home-life and on the need for women to develop expertise in homemaking duties. Motherhood acquired a new prestige as a career. Therefore, it ought not to be surprising that, in the aftermath of winning the vote, all the traditional barriers to female participation in extra-familial activities remained. The legislators who gave women the vote recognized that the reform necessitated no radical revision of sex roles. And the suffragists themselves in the main agreed. The takeover of the suffrage movement by the social reformers therefore had serious repercussions. The reform became moderate in their hands. It offered women a new political status and it raised public awareness of the mothers' contribution to the race. But it reinforced sex role stereotypes which have proved difficult to remove.

The female suffragists themselves of course broke many of these stereotypes. A number of them worked in high status jobs and even those who did not work formally frequently had other important public duties. But what they personally practised, they did not preach. For the sake of the race, they eulogized the 'cult of domesticity' as loudly as their male allies. But in the end they fared none too well either. The majority moved into fields set aside especially for women, fields like kindergarten administration or juvenile reform, which seemed to suit women's assumed abilities. Even the opportunity to participate in public reform activities declined after the War. World War I dissipated the basis for philosophical idealism which lay behind the reform movement.[8] Moreover, the feeling that somehow the problem of the city had outgrown the efforts of unorganized reform resulted in surrender to the experts. Reform became institutionalized, depersonalized, and bureaucratic.[9] Unprofessional, untrained reformers seemed redundant. Once this activity was denied them, more and more women who did not have to work to support themselves or to keep their family above the poverty line took up the call to become professional housewives.

So the female suffragists did not *fail* to effect a social revolution for women; the majority never had a revolution in mind. They remained aware of the women's side of things and worked to see women better protected and better appreciated for their traditional functions. But their motivations were really determined by their membership in a social élite which saw the need to regulate society's future and hoped the family would remain the foundation of that future. They saw the world through women's eyes but not through *any* women's eyes. Their social status, their religion, and their ethnicity coloured their vision. The farm and labour women recognized this fact and refused to work with them for this very reason.

This book asks two questions – who were Canada's suffragists? and why exactly did they want women to vote? It concludes that the suffragists were predominantly members of an Anglo-Saxon, Protestant social élite, dominated by professionals and the wives of professionals, who endorsed woman suffrage as part of a larger reform programme designed to reinstate Puritan morality, Christianity, the family, and the rule of the professional. The identification with women as a separate collectivity was secondary.

Notes

PREFACE

1 I have recently written an article surveying the literature on the woman
  suffrage movement entitled 'First-Wave Feminism: History's Judgement,'
  in Norma Grieve and Patricia Grimshaw, eds *Australian Women: Feminist
  Perspectives* (Melbourne 1981).
2 Eleanor Flexner, *Century of Struggle: The Woman's Rights Movement in the
  United States*, 3rd ed (New York 1973); Catherine Cleverdon, *The Woman
  Suffrage Movement in Canada* (Toronto 1950; reprinted 1974).
3 William O'Neill, *Everyone was Brave: a history of feminism in America*, 2nd
  ed (Chicago 1971); see also Aileen Kraditor, *The Ideas of the Woman
  Suffrage Movement, 1890–1920*, 2nd ed (New York 1971).
4 Ellen du Bois, 'The Radicalism of the Woman Suffrage Movement: Notes
  Toward the Reconstruction of Nineteenth-Century Feminism,' *Feminist
  Studies* Fall 1975, 63–71. See also du Bois, *Feminism and Suffrage: The Emergence of an Independent Woman's Movement in America, 1848–1869* (Ithaca
  1978).
5 Daniel Scott Smith, 'Family Limitation, Sexual Control and Domestic
  Feminism in Victorian America,' in L. Banner and M. Hartman, eds,
  Clio's Consciousness Raised (New York 1974); Linda Kealey, ed, *A Not
  Unreasonable Claim: Women and Reform in Canada, 1880's–1920's* (Toronto
  1979).
6 Wayne Roberts, '"Rocking the Cradle for the World": The New Woman
  and Maternal Feminism, Toronto, 1877–1914,' in Kealey, chapter 1; see
  also Roberts, *Honest Womanhood: Feminism, Femininity and Class Consciousness among Toronto Working Women, 1893 to 1914* (Toronto 1976).

INTRODUCTION

1 Refer to Catherine Cleverdon's work, *The Woman Suffrage Movement in
  Canada*, for details about Canada's suffrage organizations and the precise

dates of the suffrage victories. This study hopes to avoid needlessly repeating Cleverdon's material and to concentrate on what she left to others: specifically the ideas of the men and women who campaigned for votes for women. French-Canadian women have been left out of this analysis because their victory came so much later, but it is interesting to note that a recent study by Marie Lavigne, Yolande Pinard, and Jennifer Stoddart suggests striking parallels between the French-Canadian and English-Canadian movements. Marie Lavigne et al, 'The Fédération Nationale Saint-Jean-Baptiste and the Women's Movement in Quebec,' in Kealey, chapter 4.

2 Guy Rocher, *A General Introduction to Sociology* (Toronto 1972), 452. The nature of the available research material dictated the scope of the study and limited it to an examination of the suffrage élite, the Presidents, Vice-Presidents, and most active members.

3 These statistics are based upon the identification of some two-thirds of Canada's 200 most active suffragists, including 156 women and 44 men. Tables showing the breakdown of these figures appear on pages 6 and 7. It has been assumed that women for whom no occupation could be found were housewives.

4 The educational background of 8 men and 73 women could not be discovered. A few women fall into rather unusual categories: one was trained in a convent, one had only a high school education, one took a course preparatory to becoming a Sanitary Inspector.

5 'Middle-class' is used simply to designate that the suffragists were neither, in the main, independently wealthy nor engaged in manual labour. According to E.P. Thompson, 'class happens when some men, as a result of common experiences (inherited or shared) feel and articulate the identity of their interests as between themselves and as against other men whose interests are different from (and usually opposed to) theirs.' E.P. Thompson, *The Making of the English Working Class* (London 1963), 9. This study shows that the suffragists did think of themselves in these terms at times. But the category 'middle class' must be used loosely since this largely urban professional and entrepreneurial élite excluded other groups commonly considered middle-class. Shopkeepers were a distinct minority. Farmers also tended to keep aloof from the suffrage societies.

6 Among 28 male executive members, 16 were born in Canada, 8 came from Britain and 1 from the United States. Of 114 female executive members, 41 were Canadian-born, 9 were British, and 8 came from the United States.

7 A functional designation used to indicate British birth, Britain including Scotland and Ireland, or descendants of those of British birth. A.H. Murray, ed, *New English Dictionary on Historical Principles* (Oxford 1933).

8 See table 3 for a detailed breakdown.

9 Twelve men belonged to the Dominion Alliance or the Royal Templars while forty women were in the Woman's Christian Temperance Union.

10 It is impossible to list the many societies which had suffragists as mem-

bers, but the names of several other groups will confirm the types of reform which attracted them: the Single Tax Association, the Progressive Club, the Progressive Thought Club, Working Girls' Club, Household League, Social Science Club, Children's Aid, Winnipeg Humane Society, Foundling and Baby Hospital, World Children's Humane League, Free Kindergarten Association, Home and School Movement, Association for the Promotion of Technical Education, Women's Cooperative Guild and Calgary Consumers' League.

11 Four belonged to Playgrounds Associations, three to Child Welfare Societies, two to Charity Organization Societies, several to Progressive Clubs, Public Ownership Leagues, Single Tax Associations, Direct Legislation Societies, City Improvement Leagues, and City Planning Committees.

12 Wendy Mitchinson, 'The W.C.T.U.: "For God, Home and Native Land": A Study in Nineteenth-Century Feminism,' in Kealey, chapter 7. See also Malcolm G. Decarie, 'The Prohibition Movement in Ontario, 1894–1916,' PHD thesis (Queen's 1972); Robert I. Maclean, 'A "Most Effectual" Remedy: Temperance and Prohibition in Alberta, 1875–1915,' MA thesis (University of Calgary 1969); John H. Thompson, 'The Prohibition Question in Manitoba,' MA thesis (University of Manitoba 1969).

13 Terrence R. Morrison, 'The Child and Urban Social Reform in late Nineteenth Century Ontario, 1875–1900,' PHD thesis (University of Toronto 1970), 215–73.

14 In Neil Sutherland's study, *Children in English-Canadian Society: Framing the Twentieth Century Consensus* (Toronto 1976), familiar suffrage personalities like Emily Stowe, James Hughes and his wife Ada Maureau, Judge Helen Gregory MacGill of British Columbia, and Eliza Ritchie of Halifax all appear. Other progressive personalities in the book who endorsed female suffrage included the Methodist minister Albert Carman, the campaigner for child welfare J.J. Kelso, and the health reformer Peter H. Bryce. The same and other common personalities appear in Morrison, and in Roberts, 'Rocking the Cradle,' in Kealey, chapter 1.

15 Peter G. Filene, 'An Obituary for "The Progressive Movement,"' *American Quarterly*, Spring 1970.

16 See, for example, Morrison, 55; Mitchinson, 151; Kealey, Introduction; Sutherland, 17. Also refer to Alison Prentice, *The School Promoters: Education and Social Class in Mid-Nineteenth Century Upper Canada* (Toronto 1971), 67ff; Paul Boyer, *Urban Masses and Moral Order in America, 1820–1920* (Cambridge, Massachusetts 1978), 33ff; Harold Perkin, *The Origins of Modern English Society, 1780–1880* (London 1969), Preface.

17 David P. Thelen, 'Social Tensions and the Origins of Progressivism,' *Journal of American History*, Sept. 1969; Jack Tager, 'Progressives, Conservatives, and the Theory of the Status Revolution,' *Mid-America*, July 1966.

18 Robert H. Wiebe, *The Search for Order, 1877–1920* (London 1967), Preface.

19 Michael Bliss, 'A Living Profit: Studies in the Social History of Canadian Business, 1883–1911,' PHD thesis (University of Toronto 1972), Introduction.

20 R.C. Brown and Ramsay Cook, *Canada, 1896–1921: A Nation Transformed* (Toronto 1974).
21 J.M.S. Careless, ed, *The Canadians, 1867–1967*, vol 1 (Toronto 1967), 150–210.
22 Morrison, table 2, 27, 28.
23 Gustavus Myers, *History of Canadian Wealth*, vol 1 (Chicago 1914), xxxi.
24 Brown and Cook, 309.
25 Boyer, 280; Prentice, 180.
26 Boyer, 175ff.
27 Morrison, 51; Sutherland, 17, 237.
28 Rocher, 103.

CHAPTER ONE

1 In 1881 there were 2,126,415 women aged ten and over to 2,179,703 men; in 1901, 2,603,170 to 2,715,436; and in 1921, 4,253,341 to 4,522,512. Between 1904 and 1913 male immigrants outnumbered female by at least two to one. M.C. Urquhart and K.A.H. Buckley, eds, *Historical Statistics of Canada* (Toronto 1965), 17, 25.

2 In 1891 approximately 11 per cent of the female population over age ten worked. The percentage crept up by 1 per cent in 1901, another 2 per cent in 1911 and by 1921 15.2 per cent were employed. *Census of Canada*, table IV, xiv.

3 Britain's population – number of females to every 1000 males: 1801 – 1,057; 1851 – 1,042; 1871 – 1,054; 1891 – 1,063; 1911 – 1,068

4 Number of males to 100 females in major Eastern cities:

	1891	1911	1921
Montreal	90.5	100.4	94.7
Toronto	94	98.1	92.6
Ottawa	91	92	87

Census of Canada, 1921, p 340.

5 Number of males to 100 females in major Western cities:

	1891	1911	1921
Winnipeg	109.5	120.7	100.4
Calgary	124	155	101
Vancouver	187.5	149.9	113.1

Census of Canada, 1921, p 340.

6 Number of females to every 1000 male workers:

	1891	1911	1921
Quebec	134	183	215
Ontario	149	185	211
Manitoba	85	142	171
Nova Scotia	168	164	184
British Columbia	68	88	131

Census of Canada, 1921, xiv.

7 In 1911, 38.1 per cent of women gainfully employed in Canada were in domestic service; 27 per cent were in manufacturing. *Census of Canada*, 1921, xvi.

8 Ibid.

9 *Census of Canada*, 1915, pp 92–9.

10 Urquhart and Buckley, 594.

11 Women lawyers were recognized in New Brunswick in 1906, in British Columbia and Manitoba in 1912, and in Nova Scotia in 1917.

12 *B.C. Federationist*, 16 January 1914.

13 Woman's Edition, *Montreal Herald*, 23 Nov. 1913, p 4.

14 A complaint by Francis Marion Beynon, Woman's Editor of the *Grain Growers' Guide* and an active member of the Manitoba Political Equal Franchise League. *Grain Growers' Guide*, 3 Sept. 1913.

15 Melvin Richter, *The Politics of Conscience: T.H. Green and his Age* (London 1964), 29.

16 University of Waterloo, Elizabeth Smith-Shortt Papers, *Diary*, vol II.

17 Rocher, 41.

18 Approximately 25 per cent of Canadian male and female suffragists came into the movement through the WCTU and other temperance societies. The relationship between the WCTU and the suffrage movement is treated in depth in chapter 4.

19 At the local, the provincial, and the federal level, the Council was composed of two delegates from every existing woman's society, including the suffrage associations. The representatives were asked to forget their partisan interests, but somehow the issue of woman suffrage came up for frequent discussion.

20 National Council of Women of Canada, *Reports of Annual Meetings*, 1910, p 100.

21 Wilfrid Laurier University Archives, Emily Stowe Papers, scrapbook III, untitled, undated newspaper clipping, c 1890.

22 Montreal Women's Club, *Annual Reports*, 1893, 1894, 1895, 1901.

23 Mrs Edwards moved West and joined the Alberta suffrage movement; Helen R.Y. Reid was the daughter of the founder, Mrs Robert Reid; Margaret Polson Clark Murray, the wife of McGill professor John Clark Murray, founded the Imperial Order of the Daughters of the Empire; Dr Grace Ritchie became Dr Ritchie-England after her marriage to Dr Frank England.

24 Of a sample of 156 women, educational information was available for 83.

25 For example, Dundas Ladies' College in Hamilton, founded in 1857; the Wesleyan Ladies' College, Hamilton, 1859; the Ontario Ladies' College, Whitby, 1874; Alexandra College, Belleville, 1871; Presbyterian Ladies' College, Brantford; Stanstead Wesleyan College, Quebec; Bishop Strachan School; Havergal College; and many others. 'Methodist Educational Institutions,' *Methodist Magazine*, May 1879, p 399.

26 The Montreal Ladies' Education Association, linked to McGill, existed from 1871 to 1882; the Toronto Association operated from 1869 to 1877.

27 Girton and Newnham in Cambridge; Somerville and Lady Margaret Hall in Oxford.
28 S. Woolf, 'Women at McGill: The Ladies' Education Association of Montreal,' unpublished history paper, McGill University 1971, p 2.
29 McGill University Archives, J.W. Dawson Papers, correspondence with John Clark Murray re Higher Education of Women, Annual University Lecture, 1880–1.
30 McGill University Archives, John Clark Murray Papers, *Montreal Witness*, 1 May 1888.
31 Carlotta Hacker, *The Indomitable Lady Doctors* (Toronto 1974).
32 For example, Emily Stowe first worked as a teacher. Nine suffragists of 156 attended Normal School first and then proceeded to study for a university degree.
33 Richter, 29ff.
34 Ibid.
35 Carrie Derick, 'In the 80's,' *Old McGill*, 1927, p 350.
36 Carrie Derick, 'Address to the Delta Sigma Society,' *McGill Fortnightly*, 10 Feb. 1896, p 1190.
37 O'Neill, chapter 1.

CHAPTER TWO

1 Kraditor, chapter 3. A recent study by William Leach suggests that Kraditor's two-wave model is too rigid and that even in the United States the two arguments, natural rights and woman's moral superiority, were offered on behalf of women's rights throughout the campaign. This was definitely the case in Canada. William Leach, *True Love and Perfect Union* (London 1981), 8.
2 Ibid, 1.
3 Wilfrid Laurier University Archives (WLUA), Emily Stowe Papers, article on Emily Stowe by Miss Maryard-Smith, undated.
4 Emily Stowe's life established a pattern noticeable in the histories of several suffrage leaders. The women began in a profession, frequently teaching. They married and retired to the home. Several years and several children later they re-entered the job market. Often the death or ill health of their husbands forced them to return to work.
5 Susan B. Anthony wrote Dr Stowe's daughter, Augusta Stowe-Gullen, on the death of her mother in 1903: 'How well I remember her way back at Dr. Lozier's in 1867 and 68 in New York.' Clemence S. Lozier, a well-known defender of women's higher education, headed the New York Women's Medical College. Significantly, Kraditor considers Anthony and Stanton two principal spokesmen for the radical phase of American suffrage history. Personal contacts like these were crucial for the spread of the movement. WLUA, Emily Stowe Papers, scrapbook III, Anthony to Stowe-Gullen, 25 May 1903.

6 Ibid, scrapbook IV, Stowe to the editor of the *Toronto Globe*: 29 Nov. 1877; Stowe lecture on 'Woman's Sphere,' c 1877.
7 W. Stewart Wallace, *The Macmillan Dictionary of Canadian Biography* (Toronto 1967), 167.
8 Donald A. McDonnell, warden of Kingston Penitentiary in 1861, died in 1879. Richard B. Splane, *Social Welfare in Ontario, 1791–1893* (Toronto 1965), 185.
9 Marc Le Terreur, ed, *Dictionary of Canadian Biography, 1871 to 1880* (Toronto 1881), 469.
10 Maria Pollard, the daughter of Rev William Pollard and Mrs Pollard, the first President of the WCTU, became Mrs Gordon Grant, the President of the Victoria Political Equality League.
11 Anna Leonowens won her reputation as author of *An English Governess at the Court of Siam*. Eliza Ritchie, born in Halifax in 1856, the daughter of Judge Thomas Ritchie of the Nova Scotia Supreme Court, graduated from Dalhousie and Cornell, and became a Professor at Wellesley College between 1890 and 1900.
12 Cleverdon, 160.
13 Edith Jessie Archibald, the daughter of the former Attorney-General of Newfoundland, later the Consul-General at New York, joined the new society. Previously she had been active in the Dominion and Provincial WCTU, the NCW, and the Halifax Local Council. A second newcomer, Mary Russell Chesley, had served for four years as President of the Nova Scotia WCTU. John Leonard, ed, *Woman's Who's Who of America* (New York 1914), 54, 175.
14 Public Archives of Canada (PAC), John Macdonald Papers, Curzon to Macdonald, 29 May 1884.
15 See Frank Hatheway in *Canadian Parliamentary Guide*, 1912, p 433.
16 Iceland had an early suffrage movement. White, Nordic, and Protestant, the Icelanders co-operated in 1894 and again in 1916 with Canada's native suffragists.
17 Like Emily Stowe, Amelia Yeomans had been married for several years and only turned to medicine after her husband's death in 1878. She also became determined that her daughter, Lillian, would become a doctor. Together they attended Ann Arbor Medical School in the 1880s. Cleverdon, 50; H.J. Morgan, *Canadian Men and Women of the Time* (Toronto 1898), 1108.
18 George Maclean Rose, *A Cyclopedia of Canadian Biography* (Toronto 1886), 391, 82; H.J. Morgan, *Canadian Men and Women of the Time* (Toronto 1912), 1097.
19 Morgan 1912, pp 347, 498.
20 Morgan 1912, p 785; Stewart Wallace, 49. Women who used only their husbands' names or initials publicly will be referred to in that form.
21 Morgan 1898, p 157; Ontario WCTU, *Report*, 1878.
22 WLUA, Stowe Papers, scrapbook III, address by Emily Stowe, c 1890.

23 Indicative of the American influence in this period, a portrait of Susan B. Anthony hung over the middle of the platform at the 1889 inauguration of the DWEA.

24 Propertied widows and spinsters received the school suffrage shortly after the municipal vote in 1883 and won the right to sit as members of the School Board at the same time. Edith M. Luke, 'Woman Suffrage in Canada,' *Canadian Magazine*, Toronto 1895, p 329.

25 Ibid, 330.

26 MPs James Armstrong, John Waters, Andrew B. Ingram; alderman John Baxter; former Mayor of Toronto James Beatty; Minister of Education Hon George W. Ross; Commissioner of Crown Lands Hon A.S. Hardy; Minister of Agriculture Hon Mr Drury; the labour reformer Alexander Whyte Wright; and three prohibitionist clergymen, Rev Manly Benson, Rev Alexander Sutherland, and Rev William Robert Parker – all attended the 1889 organizational meeting of the DWEA.

27 Morgan 1898, pp 959, 594.

28 Morgan 1912, p 984.

29 Including Hattie Stevens, President of the Toronto WCTU in 1906; Mrs A. Vance, Vice-President of the Toronto WCTU in 1905; Lottie Wiggins, Superintendent of the Franchise Department for the Ontario WCTU, 1898–1900; Mrs Fred C. Ward, Franchise Superintendent for the Ontario WCTU, 1891; Mrs F.S. Spence; and Letitia Youmans, President and founder of the WCTU in Canada.

30 American suffragists organized the meeting in 1893 which led to the formation of the American National Council and the International Council of Women. Lady Aberdeen, ed, *The International Congress of Women* (London 1889), 96.

31 NCW, *Report*, 1894, p 172; 1895, p 263; Local Council of Women of Montreal, *Report*, 1897, p 7.

32 Morgan 1912, p 458.

33 University of Toronto Archives (UTA), Flora Macdonald Denison Papers, collection of newspaper clippings, Women's Section of the Toronto *Star Weekly*: 21 March 1914.

34 Ibid, scrapbook , untitled, undated clipping; *Toronto World*: 2 May 1909.

35 Ibid, 'Flora Macdam's Karma,' unpublished, undated typescript.

36 Dr C.W. Parker, ed, *Who's Who and Why* (Toronto 1914), 297.

37 Beatrice Pullen-Burry, *From Halifax to Vancouver* (London 1912), 150.

38 James L. Hughes, *Equal Suffrage* (Toronto 1895), 31.

39 Nellie McClung, 'Speaking of Women,' *Maclean's Magazine*, May 1916, p 26.

40 NCW, *Report*, 1913, pp 70, 71.

41 University of Waterloo Archives, Smith-Shortt Papers, speech to a Mother's Meeting, 1913.

42 *Grain Growers' Guide*: 1 Feb. 1911.

43 *Toronto World*: 14 Dec. 1913.

44 Since 1867, Britain had sustained a non-militant suffrage group, the National Union of Woman Suffrage Societies, which believed in change through constitutional means. Disturbed by the lack of progress and infuriated by the ridicule heaped upon the women by government officials, in 1906 a small group of women decided to break new ground, employing a variety of tactics which ranged from civil disobedience to overt violence and destruction of public and private property. These 'militants,' led by Emmeline, Christabel, and Sylvia Pankhurst, called their organization the Women's Social and Political Union.

45 The militant leaders went on hunger strikes in gaol. Under the infamous Cat and Mouse Act, they could be released when they were seriously ill, only to be re-arrested once their health had improved.

46 Castell Hopkins, *Canadian Annual Review*, 1915, p 635.

47 In Hamilton on 1 November 1916, the suffragists staged a public meeting described in one newspaper report as 'fiery and energetic.' The women dressed in white, bore shields inscribed 'We Want the Vote,' and sang 'A Better Day is Coming.' *Toronto World*: 2 Nov. 1916.

48 Alice Chown, *The Stairway* (Boston 1921), 103.

49 *Toronto World*: 16 March 1913.

50 Agnes Chesley wrote a column for the *Montreal Herald*. Helena Gutteridge, the only identified working-class member of a suffrage association, wrote for the *B.C. Federationist* and became Secretary of the Vancouver Trades and Labour Council.

51 Cleverdon, 36.

52 This can be inferred from the occupations of their husbands. L.A. Hamilton was a land commissioner for the CPR; G.I.H. Lloyd and Major William Lang were both University of Toronto professors.

53 In an interview (October 1973), Merrill Denison told how his mother was blackballed from the Heliconian Club, a society for women in the arts, because she worked in business. See also Deborah Gorham, 'Flora Macdonald Denison: Canadian Feminist' in Kealey, chapter 2, p 54.

54 Mrs Denison, on the other hand, had difficulty understanding this choice. 'However estimable a woman she may be,' she felt that Lady Drummond's title had won her the position. *Toronto World*: 21 March 1914.

55 Interview with Merrill Denison, October 1973.

56 *Toronto World*: 15 March 1914.

57 Ibid, 21 March 1914.

58 Archives of Saskatchewan (A of s), Violet MacNaughton Papers, Lang to MacNaughton, 11 April 1915; NCW, *Year Book*, 1915, p 123.

59 *Toronto World*: 29 March 1914.

60 For biographical details see Morgan 1912, pp 274, 1189.

61 According to Merrill Denison, a battle royal raged between his mother and Nellie McClung, in Mrs Denison's estimation simply another 'johnny-come-lately' to the movement.

62 The NEFU and the CSA co-operated in the formation of a Suffragists' War

Auxiliary. Mrs A.B. Ormsby became President and Dr Stowe-Gullen and Constance Hamilton, representatives from each of the competing nationals, became Vice-Presidents. In a single year the Auxiliary raised over $6,000 and by 1918 had distributed over 11,000 recruiting leaflets.

63 *Toronto Globe*: 31 Oct. 1914.
64 Ibid, 23 Sept. 1914.
65 Ibid, 29 Nov. 1916.

CHAPTER THREE

1 *Toronto World*: 16 March 1913.
2 Ibid, 3 Feb. 1910.
3 Montreal Recorder R. Stanley Weir, *The Social Evil: Toleration Condemned* (Montreal 1909), 10.
4 Quebec WCTU, *Annual Report*, 1889, p 59.
5 Toronto's Medical Health Officer, C.J.O. Hastings, warned: 'There are few conditions in the slums of European cities that have not been revealed in Toronto.' Methodist Church, Department of Evangelism and Social Service, *Annual Report*, 1910, p 48.
6 Richter, 340.
7 George Watson, *The English Ideology: Studies in the Language of Victorian Politics* (London 1973), 69, 75.
8 R.B. McDowell, *British Conservatism, 1832–1914* (London 1959), 435.
9 Crane Brinton, *English Political Thought in the Nineteenth Century* (New York 1962), 21.
10 Arthur Mann, 'British Social Thought and American Reformers of the Progressive Era,' *Mississippi Valley Historical Review*, 1956, p 672.
11 Watson, 83.
12 Brinton, 96.
13 Ibid, 212
14 Richter, 271.
15 Ibid, 271, 296.
16 McDowell, 135–43.
17 Lorne Pierce, *Fifty Years of Public Service: A Life of James L. Hughes* (Toronto 1924), 153; *Toronto Sunday World*: 14 Nov. 1909; Mrs John Cox, 'Play for the People,' *McGill University Magazine*, 1908, p 628.
18 UTA, Denison Papers, *Sunset of Bon Echo*, April 1916, p 32.
19 International Congress of Women, *Report*, volume III, *Women in Professions*, 1899, p. 102.
20 NCW, *Annual Report*, 1912, p 67.
21 Mill later moved toward an open sympathy for socialism.
22 *Winnipeg Free Press*: 22 Jan. 1916.
23 *Montreal Herald*: 7 Nov. 1913; Nellie McClung, *In Times Like These* (Toronto 1972), 102. The original of this work appeared in 1915.

24 WLUA, Stowe Papers, scrapbook III, untitled newspaper clipping, June 1890; Stowe to editor of *Toronto Globe*, undated.

25 UTA, Denison Papers, collection of newspaper clippings, scrapbook I, untitled clipping dated August 1898, probably from Denison's column in the *Toronto Sunday World*.

26 Ibid, unpublished typescript, 'The Mental Atmosphere: the Unemployed and Zero Weather.'

27 *Montreal Herald*: 3 April 1911.

28 Weir, 10.

29 J.T. Copp, *Anatomy of Poverty* (Montreal 1974), 50.

30 *Grain Growers' Guide*: 20 Dec. 1916.

31 NCW, *Report*, 1897, p 224.

32 Richter, 340.

33 Gertrude Himmelfarb, *On Liberty and Liberalism: The Case of John Stuart Mill* (New York 1974), 66–70

34 Andrew Macphail, 'Women in Democracy,' *McGill University Magazine*, February 1920, p 4.

35 NCW, *Annual Report*, 1912, p 69.

36 Goldwin Smith, 'The Woman's Rights Movement,' *Canadian Monthly*, March 1872, p 259.

37 Hopkins, *Canadian Annual Review*, 1909, p 245.

38 Stephen Leacock, 'The Woman Question,' *Maclean's Magazine*, October 1915, p. 8.

39 *Montreal Daily Witness*: 13 March 1912; 13 Feb. 1913; *Toronto Globe*: 15 Feb. 1910.

40 Watson, 156.

41 James Hughes and Carrie Derick spoke out strongly on the need for an educational qualification for the ballot.

42 WLUA, Stowe Papers, scrapbook III, debate of the Women's Literary Society on the merits of universal suffrage, 1880.

43 UTA, Denison Papers, collection of newspaper clippings, scrapbook I, untitled clipping dated August, 1898.

44 *Grain Growers' Guide*: 1 Feb. 1911.

45 Canadian Women's Press Club, Edmonton Branch, *Club Women's Reports*, 1916, p 16.

46 *Montreal Daily Witness*: 8 Feb. 1912.

47 Howard Palmer, 'Response to Foreign Immigration, Nativism and Ethnic Tolerance in Alberta, 1890–1920,' MA thesis (Edmonton 1971), 105.

48 Saskatchewan Provincial Equal Franchise Board (Sask PEFB, *Minutes*, 12 Feb. 1918. Francis Marion Beynon, again an exception, believed that the more languages a person knew the better. *Grain Growers' Guide*: 6 June 1917.

49 PAC, NCW Papers, Graham to Torrington, 1 March 1913.

50 *Grain Growers' Guide*: 3 May 1911.

51 *Winnipeg Free Press*: 11 July 1914.
52 Byrne Hope Sanders, *Emily Murphy, Crusader* (Toronto 1945), 294.
53 Emily Murphy, *The Black Candle* (Toronto 1922), 30, 47.
54 Archives of Saskatchewan (A of S), MacNaughton Papers, file 18, *Equal Franchise League, 1914–1919*, 'Reasons Why Women Should be Enfranchised.'
55 PAC, Wilfrid Laurier Papers, McAlpine to Laurier, 8 Sept. 1911.
56 J.W. Bengough, *Bengough's Chalk Talks* (Toronto 1922), 93.
57 Hughes, *Equal Suffrage*, Preface.
58 *Grain Growers' Guide*: 4 Oct. 1911.
59 *Vancouver Sun*: 19 March 1913.
60 Wiebe, 145; Perkin, 255; Boyer, 234–40; Louis Galambros, 'The Emerging Organizational Synthesis in Modern American History,' *Business History Review*, 1970, p 284.
61 *Social Service Congress of Canada*, Ottawa 1914, p 281.
62 Sask. PEFB, *Minutes*, 1916, p 9.
63 A of S, MacNaughton Papers, *Equal Franchise League, 1914–1919*, Plan of Work; PAC, NCW Papers, vol 65, pamphlet entitled 'Ontario Woman Citizens' Association, 1917–1918.'
64 The membership in 1906 included the suffragists Mr F.J. Dixson, Mr D.W. Buchanan, and Mr S.J. Farmer.
65 For a discussion of municipal experiments in the period, see John C. Weaver, 'The Meaning of Municipal Reform: Toronto, 1895,' *Ontario History*, June 1974.
66 Milton Rokeach, *The Open and Closed Mind* (New York 1960), 127.

CHAPTER FOUR

1 Richard Allen, ed, *The Social Gospel in Canada*, Papers of the Inter-disciplinary Conference on the Social Gospel in Canada (Regina 1973); Anthony Madiros, *William Irvine: The Life of a Prairie Radical* (Toronto 1979).
2 The Secretary of the American Baptist Missionary Union made this clear in 1888 at the Centenary Conference on Protestant Missions of the World: 'Women's work in the foreign field must be careful to recognize the headship of man in ordering the affairs of the Kingdom of God ... "Adam first formed, then Eve" and "the head of the woman is still the man."' Alice L. Hageman, ed, *Sexist Religion and Women in the Church* (New York 1974), 168.
3 R.J.W. Selleck, *The New Education, 1870–1914* (London 1968), 81.
4 *Census of Canada*, 1921, p 768.
5 Introduction by J.W. Sparling to J.S. Woodsworth, *Strangers Within Our Gates* (Toronto 1909; reprinted 1972), 8.
6 Ibid, introduction by M. Barber, xix.
7 J.S. Woodsworth, *My Neighbor* (Toronto 1911), 101.
8 Alex R. Vidler, *A Century of Social Catholicism, 1820–1920* (London 1964).

9 Robert F. Wearmouth, *Methodism and the Working-Class Movements of England, 1800–1850* (London 1937), 271.
10 Methodist Church of Canada, 'Principles, Problems, Programme in Moral and Social Reforms,' Canadian Pamphlet Collection, #3786, p 53.
11 Allen, 6, 7.
12 Allen, 7ff.
13 Joy Parr, '"Transplanting from Dens of Iniquity": Theology and Child Emigration,' in Kealey, chapter 8, p 176.
14 Boyer, 175ff.
15 Several historians have argued that some degree of religious awareness motivated every social reformer. Melvin Richter, for example, suggests that men like T.H. Green turned to social reform because they were discouraged with the failures of the Christian Churches. Their motivation, according to Richter, was still essentially 'religious,' meaning in this context spiritual, non-materialistic, and other-worldly. Few would dispute that nineteenth-century idealists were moved by deep soul-searching and a sense of spiritual mission. Richter, 33.
16 In 1890 Rev B.F. Austin of the Canadian Methodist Church noted that women formed nearly two-thirds of the membership of the Christian Church. In 1910 the Methodist Church Department of Evangelism and Social Service reported a majority of three million girls and women in the Church. B.F. Austin, ed, *Woman; her Character, Culture, and Calling* (Toronto 1890), 210; Methodist Church, Dept. of Evangelism and Social Service, *Annual Report*, 1910–11, p 54.
17 NCW, *Women of Canada: Their Life and Their Work*, prepared for the Paris International Exhibition, 1900, p 303.
18 United Church Archives, Papers of the Presbyterian Missionary and Deaconess Training Home, W.A.J. Martin, 'The Ewart Missionary Training Home.'
19 *Herbert Symonds: A Memoir*, Compiled by Friends, Montreal 1921, p 178; Allen, 232, 15.
20 Social Service Congress of Canada, *Report of Proceedings and Addresses*, Ottawa 1914.
21 Hughes, 17.
22 Austin, 31.
23 University of Waterloo Archives, Smith-Shortt Papers, Diary, 1 March 1882.
24 McClung, *In Times Like These*, 65; Rev. James Woodsworth, *Thirty Years in the Canadian North-West* (Toronto 1917), 237.
25 Austin, Introduction.
26 Ralph Connor, *The Friendly Four and Other Stories* (New York 1926), 239.
27 Austin, 200, 375–80.
28 Woodsworth, *My Neighbor*, 60–70.
29 Rev W.H. Withrow, 'Higher Female Education,' *Methodist Magazine*, January 1875, p 24; Austin, 23, 24.

30 United Church Archives, Alexandra College Papers, printed flyer, c 1884.
31 United Church Archives, Albert Carman Papers, box 24, item 57, letter to *Globe* entitled 'Education of Girls.'
32 Austin, 31, 32.
33 Ibid, 33.
34 Rev W.H. Withrow, 'The Higher Education of Women,' in Austin, 325.
35 Beverley Harrison, 'Sexism and the Contemporary Church,' in Hagemen, 195ff.
36 *Winnipeg Free Press*: 13 June 1914.
37 World Methodist Ecumenical Conference, *Report*, 1921, pp 258–60.
38 See chapter two, p 31 for a discussion of Mrs Denison's feminist attitudes.
39 Queen's University Archives, Merrill Denison Papers, *The Sunset of Bon Echo*, issue #4, c 1916, p 27.
40 UTA, Denison Papers, Woman's Suffrage Correspondence, Programmes, and Speeches; undated speech.
41 Flora Macdonald Denison, *Mary Melville: the Psychic* (Toronto 1900), 147.
42 The theory of 'cosmic consciousness' is explained in Richard Maurice Burke, *Cosmic Consciousness* (Philadelphia 1901). Burke was one of the three Literary Executers of Horace Traubel who happened to be a friend of Mrs Denison's and a member of her Walt Whitman Club.
43 The President of the Montreal Equal Suffrage Club, Mildred Bain, J.W. Bengough, and Albert Durant Watson all belonged to the Whitman Club. Watson, a member of the DWEA, wrote *Mediums and Mystics*, a study in spiritual laws and psychic forces. Lorne Pierce, *Albert Durant Watson: An Appraisal* (Toronto 1923).

CHAPTER FIVE

1 According to Graeme Decarie, support for temperance was strongest in *rural* Ontario. Malcolm Graeme Decarie, 'The Prohibition Movement in Ontario, 1894–1916,' PHD thesis (Queen's 1972), abstract.
2 Decarie also notes that temperance attracted urban middle-class Protestants of all denominations. Ibid.
3 The anti-slavery movement filled a similar function for American women. Flexner, 41–52.
4 Decarie, passim; John H. Thompson, 'The Prohibition Question in Manitoba'; Robert Irwin Maclean, 'Temperance and Prohibition in Alberta'; Albert Hiebert, 'Prohibition in British Columbia.'
5 Joseph R. Gusfield's *Symbolic Crusade: Status Politics and the American Temperance Movement* (Urbana 1963) is the classic statement of this interpretation of prohibition. Although it is difficult to explain the entire progressive movement through 'status anxiety,' it seems clear that prohibitionists wanted to impose their values on foreigners, on the labouring classes, and in some instances on wealthy non-abstainers.
6 Ruth Spence, *Prohibition in Canada* (Toronto 1919), 38.

7 Decarie, 7–11.
8 Born Letitia Creighton on a farm in Cobourg, Ontario, Mrs Youmans attended the Cobourg Ladies' Academy, taught school at the Burlington Academy in Hamilton for two years, and moved to Picton, Ontario, where in 1850 she became principal of a Picton school. That same year she married Arthur Youmans, a widower with eight children, and dedicated the next eighteen years of her life to bringing up the family. In 1870, still a devoted wife and mother, she began her involvement in temperance work. Letitia Youmans, *Campaign Echoes* (Toronto 1893), 68, 91.
9 The Maritime provinces had a single union at this date, as did the North-West Territories.
10 According to Joseph Gusfield, 'in the Prohibition period, coercive reform emerges when the object of reform is seen as an intractable defender of another culture, someone who rejects the reformer's values and doesn't really want to change.' Gusfield, 7.
11 WCTU, Toronto District Union, *Report*, 1905–6, p 28. Propertied widows and spinsters received the municipal vote in Ontario in 1883 but married women had to wait until 1915 for the municipal privilege.
12 The heads of Franchise Departments frequently joined suffrage societies, their long, unrewarded campaign convincing them of the immediate need for female enfranchisement. For example, Mrs Jacob Spence and Annie Parker in Ontario, Mrs Gordon Grant in British Columbia, Mrs D.V. Buchanan in Manitoba and Henrietta Muir Edwards in Alberta, all one-time heads of WCTU Franchise Departments, became prominent suffragists.
13 Rev Thomas Webster, 'The Citizenship of Women,' *Methodist Magazine*, January 1894, p 151.
14 Decarie, 83.
15 Ontario WCTU, *Annual Report*, 1894, p 51.
16 Ibid, 1903, p 49. Results of the 1902 Ontario plebiscite: 199,749 for prohibition; 103,548 against.
17 The deputation brought out a respectable entourage including Mrs S.G.E. McKee (President of the Ontario WCTU), Mrs Thornley, Mrs Sara Rowell Wright (the sister of Newton Rowell), Mrs A.O. Rutherford (President of the National WCTU), Dr Augusta Stowe-Gullen, Rev Nathanial Burwash (Chancellor of Victoria University), Thomas Urquhart (Baptist Mayor of Toronto), Rev A.C. Courtice (editor of the Methodist *Christian Guardian*), and the Hon Adam Beck (a former Mayor of London, Ontario).
18 Ontario WCTU, *Report*, 1906, p 188; Mrs S.G.E. McKee, *Jubilee History of the Ontario W.C.T.U., 1877–1927* (Toronto 1928), 85.
19 According to Albert Hiebert, 'In the prairies, where many immigrants came from Central and Eastern Europe, the prohibition movement grew more quickly since in both religious and political circles it was thought urgent that an enforced minimum standard of morality was required to assist in "Canadianization" of the foreigner.' Hiebert, 6.
20 Thompson, 28.

21 The provinces of Alberta and Saskatchewan came into existence only in 1905.

22 Emily P. Weaver, *The Canadian Woman's Annual and Social Service Directory* (Toronto 1915), 82.

23 Maclean, 25. The farmers' contribution to woman suffrage will be examined in chapter eight.

24 A of S, J.A. Calder Papers, Musselman to Calder, 6 March 1916; Calder to Musselman, 8 March 1916. Emphasis added.

25 Flexner, 337.

26 Norman MacKensie, *Women in Australia* (Melbourne 1962), 41.

27 Nellie McClung, *Purple Springs* (New York 1922), 78. According to W.L. Morton, Roblin's coolness to the temperance movement won him the valuable support of the liquor interests. W.L. Morton, *The Progressive Party in Manitoba* (Toronto 1950), 31.

28 Hopkins, *Canadian Annual Review*, 1902, p 384.

29 Youmans, 206.

30 WLUA, Stowe Papers, scrapbook III, untitled clipping, 24 Nov. 1894, re the formation of the Manitoba Equal Suffrage Club.

31 *Toronto World*: 23 April 1911.

32 In 1916 the Manitoba Political Equality League called for 'the Prohibition of the manufacture, import, or sale of intoxicants as beverages.' In 1917 the Ontario Woman Citizens' Association supported 'Dominion-wide prohibition.' The Saskatchewan Citizens' Education Board, the successor to the PEFB, passed a resolution in 1918 asking for 'permanent prohibition throughout the Dominion of Canada.' *Winnipeg Voice*: 23 June 1916; PAC, NCW Papers, Pamphlet: *The Ontario Woman Citizens' Association*, 1917; *Grain Growers' Guide*: 27 Feb. 1918.

33 Janet Giele, 'Social Change in the Feminine Role: A Comparison of Woman's Suffrage and Woman's Temperance,' PHD thesis (Radcliffe College 1961), 49, 50.

34 Ibid, 149–52.

35 Ibid.

36 Of a sample of nineteen WCTU leaders, ten or 52.6 per cent attended Ladies' Academies or received private tutoring compared to only 11 per cent (17 of 156) of the female suffrage leaders.

37 WLUA, Stowe Papers, scrapbook IV, undated (c 1877) letter to the editor of the *Globe* from Emily Stowe.

38 Ibid, letters to *Globe* from Letitia Youmans and other members of the WCTU.

39 Decarie, 165, 340.

40 Dominion Alliance, Ontario branch, *Minutes*, 1896, p 31; Benjamin W. Richardson, *Public School Temperance* (Toronto 1887), 98.

41 Decarie.

42 Quebec WCTU, *Report*, 1885, p 21; 1903, p 47; Ontario WCTU, *Report*, 1905, p 58; 1907, p 44; 1909, p 27.

43 Although the upper class are never precisely identified, they seem to belong to an independently wealthy, Canadian aristocracy, composed perhaps of millionaires and established families. At any rate, the middle classes who filled the temperance societies saw themselves as a group distinct from this leisure class.

44 For the statistical computations, refer to my PHD thesis of the same name as this book, completed at McGill University in 1976, appendix XIII.

45 Ibid, appendix XIV.

46 *Toronto World*: 19 Oct. 1915; McClung's address to the Toronto Women's Canadian Club.

47 Austin, 400.

48 Hopkins, 1911, pp 368–9. Louise Crummy McKinney, born in Ontario, educated at Smith's Falls Model School, began a teaching career at age eighteen. At twenty-six she began work as an organizer for the WCTU in Dakota where she lived for three years. In 1896 she married James McKinney and in 1903 moved to Alberta. There she became first President of the Alberta WCTU. In 1917 Mrs McKinney was elected to the federal legislature as a Non-Partisan candidate.

49 Giele, 190.

50 Ibid.

51 Of Canada's 114 female executive members, some 63 per cent were either journalists, doctors, or teachers. In the United States, by contrast, of 49 suffrage leaders 16 per cent were journalists or authors, none were doctors, and 8 per cent were lawyers. A solid 49 per cent of the American leaders were described as either philanthropists or public lecturers, compared to only 4 per cent in the Canadian movement.

52 Giele, chapter 5. Joseph Gusfield comes to a similar conclusion about the WCTU's declining social pre-eminence: 'the socio-economic status of the local leadership has diminished during the period 1885–1950. There has been a relatively steady decrease in the percentage of professional people, proprietors, managers, and officials and a relatively steady increase in the skilled and unskilled groups.' Joseph Gusfield, 'Social Structure and Moral Reform: A Study of the Woman's Christian Temperance Union,' *American Journal of Sociology*, Nov. 1955–6, p 228.

53 Decarie, 312.

54 Ontario WCTU, *Report*, 1913, p 110.

CHAPTER SIX

1 Boyer, 190–5. See also Donald K. Pickens, *Eugenics and the Progressives* (Nashville 1968), chapter 1.

2 *Toronto World*: 23 Oct. 1909.

3 WLUA, Stowe Papers, scrapbook III, clipping from *Toronto Empire*: 1 Feb. 1889.

4 Child Welfare Exhibition, *Souvenir Handbook*, 8–22 Oct. 1912.

5 Ontario Commission on Unemployment, *Report*, 1917, p 27.

6 *Toronto World*: 10 Nov. 1907.

7 Victoria College Library, Stowe Papers, scrapbook VI, printed flyer, 'Votes for Women! The Woman's Reason.' Emphasis added.

8 *Montreal Gazette*: 27 March 1912.

9 *Industrial Banner*: 18 Oct. 1912; A of S, MacNaughton Papers, Equal Franchise League, 1914–19, Plan of Work; PAC, NCW Papers, volume 65, pamphlet: *Ontario Woman Citizens' Association, 1917–1918*.

10 *Toronto Globe*: 18 Sept. 1914.

11 Social Service Congress of Canada, Ottawa 1914, pp 119–20.

12 Susan E. Houston, 'Victorian Origins of Juvenile Delinquency: A Canadian Experience,' *History of Education Quarterly*, Fall 1972, p 254.

13 Selleck, 307.

14 See note 9.

15 Details of Hughes' life from Bruce N. Carter, 'James L. Hughes and the Gospel of Education,' Doctor of Education thesis (University of Toronto 1966).

16 Selleck, 180.

17 Carter, 256.

18 Selleck, 307.

19 Woman's Edition, *Montreal Witness*: 15 May 1909, p 27. This special issue of the *Witness* was actually sponsored by the Parks and Playgrounds Association.

20 *Toronto World*: 26 June 1910.

21 Robert M. Stamp, 'The Campaign for Technical Education in Ontario, 1876–1914,' PHD thesis (University of Western Ontario 1970), 28.

22 Selleck, 119.

23 WLUA, Stowe Papers, scrapbook III, undated (c 1895) letter to editor of *Toronto Mail* from Emily Stowe.

24 Carter, 54.

25 NCW, *Report*, 1902, p 117.

26 Relative rate per 1000 population of marriages in cities of Ontario:

	1883	1890	1892
Toronto	11.3	10.0	8.5
Hamilton	11.3	9.6	8.2
Ottawa	13.9	18.1	10.1
Kingston	11.7	9.6	7.9
London	13.6	10.4	8.7

Morrison, 28.

27 Mary Q. Innis, *The Clear Spirit* (Toronto 1966), 108; NCW, *Women of Canada*, 110; *Grain Growers' Guide*: 14 Oct. 1914; *McGill Daily*: 1 Oct. 1918.

28 *Winnipeg Free Press*: 8 April 1916.

29 *Grain Growers' Guide*: 27 Sept. 1911.

30 The proportion of domestics in the work-force declined steadily from 51.9 per cent in 1891 to 38.1 per cent in 1911 to 27.5 per cent in 1921. *Census of Canada*, 1921, xvi.
31 University of Waterloo Archives, Elizabeth Smith-Shortt Papers, Sonia Leathes to Elizabeth Shortt, 20 Dec. 1913.
32 Mrs James L. Hughes, the Toronto suffragist, was even willing to 'give the servant a dignified position' in order to encourage more women to become domestics. NCW, *Report*, 1901, p 117.
33 Alice Chown, 'The Supplement of Higher Education for Women,' *Methodist Magazine*, Nov. 1901, p 444.
34 NCW, *Report*, 1904, p 121.
35 Lola Martin Burgoyne, *A History of the Home and School Movement in Ontario* (Toronto 1935), introduction.
36 Elsie Gregory MacGill, *My Mother, the Judge* (Toronto 1955), 121.
37 A of S, MacNaughton Papers, Equal Franchise League, Plan of Work; PAC, NCW Papers, volume 65, Pamphlet: *Ontario Woman Citizens' Association, 1917–1918*.
38 *Winnipeg Free Press*: 3 July 1915.
39 *Montreal Gazette*: 21 Dec. 1915.
40 Sask. PEFB, *Minutes*, 12 Feb. 1918.
41 Montreal Local Council of Women, Twenty-First Anniversary *Reports, 1893–1915*, 15. For more detail on compulsory medical school inspection, refer to Neil Sutherland, 'To Create a Strong and Healthy Race: School Children in the Public Health Movement,' *History of Education Quarterly*, Fall 1972, pp 304–33.
42 Morgan 1912, p 274.
43 Christopher Lasch, *The New Radicalism in America: The Intellectual as a Social Type* (New York 1965), 161.
44 Wayne Roberts in Kealey, chapter 1.
45 Veronica Strong-Boag, 'Canada's Women Doctors: Feminism Constrained,' in Kealey, chapter 5, p 129.
46 Dorothy Ross, 'Socialism and American Liberalism: Academic Social Thought in the 1880's,' *Perspectives in American History*, 1977–8, pp 62ff.
47 WLUA, Stowe Papers, scrapbook III, clipping, *Toronto News*: 31 Dec. 1895.
48 Dick McDonald, *Mugwump Canadian: The Merrill Denison Story* (Montreal 1973), 151.
49 Woman's Edition, *Montreal Herald*: 26 Nov. 1913.
50 A of S, MacNaughton Papers, Equal Franchise League, 1914–19, Plan of Work.
51 *Grain Growers' Guide*: 4 Feb. 1914.
52 W.H. Atherton, *The History of Montreal*, vol 2 (Montreal 1914), 672–3.
53 NCW, *Report*, 1902.
54 *Winnipeg Free Press*: 2 May 1914.
55 Woman's Edition, *Vancouver Sun*: 19 March 1913, pp 12, 20.

56 Wiebe, 181.
57 Brown and Cook, 106.
58 Atherton, 672.
59 See chapter three, p 56.
60 Chown, *The Stairway*, 37.
61 On one occasion Chown confessed: 'I am a snob, a first-class snob. The only difference between me and other snobs is that I am conscious I am a snob.' Ibid, 285.
62 NCW, *Report*, 1901, p 101.

CHAPTER SEVEN

1 Ronald Hyam, *Britain's Imperial Century, 1815–1914* (London 1976); G.R. Searle, *The Quest for National Efficiency* (London 1971).
2 Bernard Semmel, *Imperialism and Social Reform* (Cambridge, Massachusetts 1960).
3 G.R. Searle, *Eugenics and Politics in Britain, 1900–1914* (London 1976), 32.
4 Annie Parker, 'Woman in Nation Building' in Austin, *Woman*, 465.
5 The theory of acquired characteristics had been unchallenged until the middle of the nineteenth century. In 1869 Galton published *Hereditary Genius* which stressed the hereditary aspects of human existence and society. In 1883 the German embryologist and geneticist August Weissman developed his 'germ-plasm' theory which completely denied the impact of environment. The rediscovery of Mendel in 1900 strengthened the allegiance to hereditary determinism. Pickens, 26; Hans Stubbe, *History of Genetics* (Cambridge, Massachusetts 1972), 176; A.H. Sturtevant, *A History of Genetics* (New York 1965), chapter 3.
6 See Pickens, passim. Also, Mark H. Haller, *Eugenics: Hereditarian Attitudes in American Thought* (New York 1963) and Kenneth M. Ludmerer, *Genetics and American Society: A Historical Appraisal* (Baltimore 1972).
7 WLUA, Stowe Papers, scrapbook III, undated (c 1897) letter from Stowe to the editor of the *Toronto Mail*.
8 UTA, Denison Papers, newspaper clippings re Woman Suffrage, scrapbook I, clipping, untitled, June 1898.
9 Mark Haller, 82.
10 *Montreal Star*: 24 October 1914.
11 Ludmerer, 10.
12 *Montreal Witness*: 12 October 1910.
13 A of S, Mrs S.V. Haight Papers, drafts of speeches, undated speech on the feeble-minded.
14 NCW, *Annual Report*, 1912, p 29.
15 Peter H. Bryce, MD, 'The Ethical Problems Underlying the Social Evil,' reprinted from the *Journal of Preventive Medicine and Sociology*, Toronto, March, 1914, p 13. Bryce was also the Chief Medical Officer for the Department of Immigration.

16 Mark Haller, 81.
17 Semmel, 46.
18 *Montreal Witness*: 12 October 1910.
19 Edward Playter, MD, 'The Physical Culture of Women,' in Austin, *Woman*, 225.
20 Dominion WCTU, *Annual Report*, 1891, Department of Heredity and Hygiene, 88.
21 John S. and Robin M. Haller, *The Physician and Sexuality in Victorian America* (Urbana 1974), 146.
22 Suse Woolf, 'Women at McGill: the Ladies' Education Association of Montreal,' McGill University, unpublished paper, 1971, p 9.
23 See chapter six, p 95.
24 See chapter six, p 90.
25 Social Service Congress of Canada, *Report of Proceedings* (Toronto 1914), 208.
26 Emily Murphy, *The Black Candle*, 307.
27 William J. Brown, MD, *Syphilis: A Synopsis* (Washington 1968), 9–11.
28 *Winnipeg Free Press*: 3 July 1915.
29 Social Service Congress, *Report*, 209.
30 Brown, 10.
31 D. Llewellyn-Jones, *Sex and Venereal Disease* (London 1974), 42.
32 Glen Petrie, *A Singular Iniquity: The Campaigns of Josephine Butler* (New York 1971).
33 Haller and Haller, 243.
34 Methodist Church, Department of Evangelism and Social Service, *Annual Report*, 1912–13, p 10.
35 Social Service Congress, *Report*, 208.
36 *Grain Growers' Guide*: 16 January 1918.
37 Michael Bliss, 'Pure Books on Avoided Subjects: Pre-Freudian Sexual Ideas in Canada,' Canadian Historical Association, *Historical Papers*, 1970, p 104.
38 WCTU, *Annual Reports*.
39 David J. Pivar, 'The New Abolitionism: The Quest for Social Purity,' PHD thesis (University of Pennsylvania 1965).
40 One volume, entitled *What a Young Man Ought to Know*, contained a sixty-page lecture on the frightful effects of venereal disease.
41 Beatrice Brigden and William Lund Clark were hired by the Canadian Methodist Church. Arthur W. Beall lectured to the schoolboys of Ontario on behalf of the WCTU. See United Church Archives, Methodist Church, Board of Evangelical and Social Service, Correspondence between Beatrice Brigden and Dr Albert Moore; also, Beatrice Brigden and William Lund Clark Papers. To an extent, the anxiety about the public's sexual excesses went beyond the fear about the transmission of sexual disease. Victorian vitalist physiology maintained that the body contained a limited amount of expendable energy and therefore unrestrained sexual activity threatened to deplete the body's resources. Bliss, 104.

42 Social Service Congress, *Report*, 213.
43 WLUA, Stowe Papers, scrapbook IV, undated (c 1877) newspaper clipping.
44 *Winnipeg Free Press*: 19 August 1916.
45 Chown, 114.
46 Sask. PEFB, *Minutes of Meetings*, 18 February 1916.
47 UTA, Denison Papers, unpublished typescript, 'The White Slave Traffic,' nd.
48 *Montreal Herald*, Woman's Edition, 26 November 1913, p 24.
49 *B.C. Federationist*: 17 October 1916.
50 *Toronto World*: 15 January 1911. Emphasis added.
51 *Winnipeg Free Press*: 7 October 1916.
52 *Montreal Herald*: 24 September 1913.
53 *Grain Growers' Guide*: 26 February 1913.
54 Helen Gregory MacGill, *Daughters, Wives, and Mothers in British Columbia: Some Laws Regarding Them* (Vancouver 1913), 31.
55 Haller and Haller, xii.
56 Bliss, 103.
57 *Grain Growers' Guide*: 14 August 1912; *Winnipeg Free Press*: 28 August 1915; *Toronto World*: 31 October 1909; *Montreal Herald*, Woman's Edition, 26 November 1913, p 17.
58 Chown, 114.
59 C. Rover, *Love, Morals and the Feminists* (London 1970). Most Canadian suffragists did not even discuss the subject as it was considered socially taboo.
60 J.A. and Olive Banks, *Feminism and Family Planning in Victorian England* (New York 1964).

CHAPTER EIGHT

1 Western women campaigned for a dower law to guarantee a married woman a one-third interest in a deceased husband's estate. In 1911 Ada Muir, Secretary of the Women's Labour League, led the deputation which included the prominent suffragists Nellie McClung, Mrs M. Iveson, and Mrs H.E. Kelly. *Grant Growers' Guide*: 1 March 1911.
2 Hopkins, *Canadian Annual Review*, 1902, p 87.
3 Martin Robin, *Radical Politics and Canadian Labour, 1880–1930* (Kingston 1968), 31.
4 *Toronto Globe*: 29 Sept. 1916. Alice Klein and Wayne Roberts also draw attention to the fact that unions co-operated with middle-class reformers because of their fear of competition from women. 'Besieged Innocence: The "Problem" and Problems of Working Women – Toronto, 1896–1914' in Janice Acton, Penny Goldsmith, and Bonnie Shepard, eds, *Women at Work: Ontario, 1850–1930* (Toronto 1974), 220.
5 *Winnipeg Voice*: 1 Oct. 1915; 20 Dec. 1912.
6 Emily Murphy, *Seeds of Pine* (Toronto 1914), 259.
7 Chown, 146, 153.

8 *Toronto World*: 7 Dec. 1913.
9 *B.C. Federationist*: 17 Oct. 1913; 16 Jan. 1914.
10 *Winnipeg Voice*: 18 Feb. 1910; 28 Oct. 1910.
11 Ibid, 20 Dec. 1907; 19 July 1907.
12 Ibid, 18 Sept. 1918.
13 No details are available about the cause or nature of the strike. Lionel G. Orlikow, 'A Survey of the Reform Movement in Manitoba,' MA thesis (University of Manitoba 1955), 188.
14 *Industrial Banner*: 26 Nov. 1915.
15 *B.C. Federationist*: 11 Feb. 1916.
16 *Industrial Banner*: 10 Aug. 1917; 5 March 1918.
17 Ibid, 31 May 1918.
18 Traditionally Canadian historians have described the West – that is, the Prairie Provinces – as a single and separate entity exhibiting a distinct Western regional consciousness. It is true that between the settling of Manitoba in the 1870s and the creation of Alberta and Saskatchewan in 1905, Westerners did begin to conceive of themselves as a group apart. Recent historiography, however, suggests that it is incorrect to think of the West in such a monolithic fashion and that geographical and class tensions undermined the West's homogeneity. More specifically, an urban-rural conflict existed in the West, based upon an even deeper occupational rift between the farming population and the urban bourgeoisie. George F. Stanley, 'The Western Canadian Mystique' in David P. Gagan, *Prairie Perspectives* (Toronto 1969), 6; J.M.S. Careless, 'Aspects of Urban Life in the West, 1870–1914' in A.W. Rasporich and H.C. Klassen, eds, *Prairie Perspectives*, 2 (Toronto 1970–1), 28.
19 Careless, 'Aspects of Urban Life,' 25.
20 Morton, 5. See also Thomas Flanagan, 'Political Geography and the United Farmers of Alberta,' in S.M. Trofimenkoff, ed, *The Twenties in Western Canada* (Ottawa 1972), 138, 143.
21 *Grain Growers' Guide*: 31 Jan. and 7 Feb. 1913.
22 The GGA and the UFA both strongly supported prohibition.
23 *Grain Growers' Guide*: 14 Feb. 1914.
24 Ibid, 26 June 1918.
25 Eva Carter, *The History of Organized Farm Women of Alberta* (undated pamphlet), 19.
26 Manitoba Political Equality League, *Minutes*, 21 March 1914.
27 June Menzies, 'Votes for Saskatchewan Women,' in Norman Ward, ed, *Politics in Saskatchewan* (Toronto 1968), 84.
28 A of S, Zoa Haight Papers, MacNaughton to Zoa Haight, 30 March 1914.
29 Sask. PEFB, *Minutes*, 13 Feb. 1915.
30 In 1916 Mrs MacNaughton condemned the Board for neglecting her: 'So, I am still a member of this Board. Well, I have not received any minutes. There is certainly something funny about that Board.' A of S, Haight Papers, MacNaughton to Haight, 24 April 1916.

31 According to Mrs MacNaughton, neither of the Toronto-based National Suffrage Associations was really national in character. Each simply wanted to secure the affiliation of the Western provinces because of their anticipated successes in the provincial suffrage field. Ibid.
32 *Grain Growers' Guide*: 2 April 1913.
33 Ibid, 11 Dec. 1918.
34 Ibid, 4 Dec. 1918.
35 Annie Walker, *Fifty Years of Achievement* (Ontario 1948), 10.
36 A of S, MacNaughton Papers, Irene Parlby to Violet MacNaughton, 14 March 1916.
37 M. Viola Powell, *Forty Years Agrowing: the History of the Ontario Women's Institutes* (Ontario 1941), 18; NCW, *Report*, 1903, p 24.
38 *Farm and Ranch Review*: 21 Feb. 1916.
39 S.E.D. Shortt, 'Social Change and Political Crisis in Rural Ontario: the Patrons of Industry, 1889–1896,' in Donald Swainson, ed, *Oliver Mowat's Ontario* (Toronto 1972), 234.
40 A of S, Haight Papers, MacNaughton to Haight, 23 July 1914.
41 *Grain Growers' Guide*: 11 Dec. 1918. The Institutes tried to introduce a plan to divide the territory between themselves and the UFWA, restricting the UFWA to areas where no Institutes existed. Parlby refused because she feared that, with government support, the Institutes would soon out-number UFWA locals.
42 PAC, Robert Borden Papers, pamphlet #84570, *The Woman's Party, Ontario, 1918,* 'Victory, National Security, and Progress.'
43 *Grain Growers' Guide*: 16 Oct. 1918.
44 Donald Page, 'The Development of a Western Canadian Peace Movement,' in Trofimenkoff, 90.
45 *Grain Growers' Guide*: 16 Oct. 1918.
46 Ibid.
47 Ibid, 4 Dec. 1918.
48 Ibid, 13 Nov. 1918.
49 A of S, MacNaughton Papers, Subject File: Woman's Party, 1918–1919, Hamilton to MacNaughton, 16 Dec. 1918.
50 PAC, Robert Borden Papers, pamphlet #84570.
51 *Grain Growers' Guide*: 11 Dec. 1918.
52 *Industrial Banner*: 22 Nov. 1918.
53 Michael Bliss, 'The Protective Impulse: An Approach to the Social History of Oliver Mowat's Ontario,' in Swainson, 181.

CHAPTER NINE

1 Constance Rover, *Woman's Suffrage and Party Politics in Britain, 1866–1914* (Toronto 1967), 101. A quotation from Harold Laski, a member of the Montreal Suffrage Association in 1915.
2 Sir Joseph Pope, *Sir John A. Macdonald, Prime Minister of Canada*, volume 2, undated.

3 Sir Joseph Pope, *The Day of Sir John Macdonald* (Toronto 1920), 138.
4 Hansard, *House of Commons Debates*, 1885, pp 1388–9.
5 Hansard 1885, p 1391.
6 Ibid, 1399.
7 PAC, John A. Macdonald Papers, Hamilton Wilcox to Macdonald, 3 June 1888; Macdonald to Wilcox, August 1888; Hansard 1885, pp 1388, 1389.
8 *Montreal Herald*: 28 April 1885.
9 Ibid.
10 Hansard 1888, p 1444.
11 For details about the provincial suffrage battles, see Cleverdon.
12 Morton, 122.
13 Manitoba, 28 January 1916; Saskatchewan, 14 March 1916; Alberta, 19 April 1916.
14 Cleverdon, 125, 126.
15 In 1917 Meighen received a report from Manitoba which confirmed his fears: 'In Emerson (Provencher) I would judge that the Galicians now control the constituency ... In Mountain and Manitou ... there is a full French registration as well as others. All Sisters of Charity have registered and Baird tells me that the French control Mountain. I might add Dufferin and another constituency in which there is a full French vote. In Winnipeg I understand the female vote exceeds the male by 324, a full foreign registration.' PAC, Robert Borden Papers, Colbert Locke to Meighen, 21 July 1917.
16 Ibid, Meighen to Borden, 4 October 1916.
17 Ibid.
18 Brian D. Tennyson, 'Premier Hearst and Votes for Women,' *Ontario History*, September 1965, p 120.
19 Ibid.
20 Audrey M. Adams, 'A Study of the Use of Plebiscites and Referendums by the Province of British Columbia,' MA thesis (University of British Columbia 1958), 53.
21 Referendum results: civilian vote: 43,619 for, 18,604 against; soldiers' vote: 8,273 for, 6,002 against.
22 PAC, Borden Papers, Meighen to Borden, 14 April 1917.
23 Ibid, Borden to Meighen, 17 April 1917.
24 Francis Marion Beynon and Lillian Beynon Thomas in *Winnipeg Free Press*: 16 December 1916.
25 *Toronto World*: 21 September 1917.
26 NCW, *Year Book*, 1915, p 125.
27 *Grain Growers' Guide*: 26 January 1916.
28 According to Mrs Stevens, the Prime Minister had asked her to find out if full enfranchisement of Canada's women would guarantee conscription. Ontario WCTU, *Annual Report*, 1917, p 82.
29 *Toronto Globe*: 2 August 1917.
30 A of S, MacNaughton Papers, MacNaughton to Torrington, c 6 August 1917.

31 PAC, Borden Papers, 'Women of Canada and the War Franchise Act,' item 74783.
32 A of S, MacNaughton Papers, copy of Mrs Torrington's statement which appeared in the Toronto papers of 6 December 1917.
33 *Toronto Globe*: 22 September 1917. Mrs Hamilton's husband, L.A. Hamilton, land commissioner for the CPR, almost won the Conservative nomination in Peel in 1917.
34 *Grain Growers' Guide*: 21 February 1917; PAC, NCW, Papers, J. Wilson to Emily Cummings, 13 September 1917.
35 Montreal Suffrage Association, *Minutes*, 4 September 1917; 14 September 1917; 1 February 1918.
36 NCW, *Report*, 1918, pp 55, 58.
37 Dominion of Canada, Wartime Act, 20 September 1917; all women, 24 May 1918. Nova Scotia, 26 April 1918; New Brunswick, 17 April 1919; Prince Edward Island, 3 May 1922; Newfoundland, 13 April 1925; Quebec, 25 April 1940.
38 Montreal Suffrage Association, *Minutes*, 19 August 1914; Montreal Local Council of Women, *Twenty-First Anniversary, Reports for 1893–1915*, 80; McGill University Archives, Women's War Register.
39 A of S, MacNaughton Papers, E.E. Stores to MacNaughton, 21 September 1914.
40 Tennyson, 117.

CONCLUSION

1 Anne Anderson Perry, 'Is Women's Suffrage a Fizzle?' *Maclean's Magazine*, Feb. 1928.
2 The 1941 Census records 165,140 female to 98,783 male professionals. The breakdown in table 4, p 177, indicates where the female professionals congregated. Census of Canada, 1941, vol VII, 772.
3 Average annual earnings, male and female wage earners, manufacturing industries, are shown in table 5, p 177. Urquhart and Buckley, 100.
4 Percentage of female work force who were married: 1946 – 28.8 per cent; 1950 – 29.5 per cent; 1955 – 36.8 per cent; 1960 – 47.4 per cent; ibid, 66.
5 Percentage of full-time female undergraduate enrolment in Canadian universities: 1925 – 21 per cent; 1930 – 23.5 per cent; 1935 – 22.2 per cent; 1940 – 22.7 per cent; 1945 – 28.7 per cent; 1950 – 20.4 per cent; 1955 – 21.5 per cent; 1958 – 22.2 per cent. The high percentage in 1945 was due to the war. Ibid, 601.
6 Ibid, 602, 603.
7 In an 1882 letter to Elizabeth Smith, her sister Mauritana referred to an encounter with Dr and Mr Stowe. She derogatorily called Emily Stowe 'the biggest man of the two.' University of Waterloo Archives, Smith-Shortt Papers, Mauritana to Elizabeth Smith, 12 Feb. 1882.
8 Richter, 375.
9 Terrence Morrison, 10.

TABLE 4

	Male	Female
Schoolteachers	21,474	63,192
Nurses	198	36,135
Legal stenographers	48	3,882
Nuns and sisters	–	5,238
Surgeons and physicians	10,062	367
Lawyers	7,183	102

TABLE 5

	Male	Female
1935	$ 966	$ 570
1940	1,202	655
1945	1,739	984
1950	2,419	1,376
1955	3,267	1,833
1959	3,929	2,419

Primary Sources

MANUSCRIPT COLLECTIONS

Archives of British Columbia
    Nellie McClung, Private Papers and Correspondence
Glenbow Foundation, Calgary
    Roberta MacAdams Price, Correspondence and Documents re Personal Life
    and Career, 1911–23.
    Mrs Jean McDonald, *Memoirs*, 1877–1969
    Tom Williams, Collector, WGGA
Archives of Manitoba
    Minnie J.B. Campbell Papers
    Margaret McWilliams Papers
    T.C. Norris Papers
    Lillian Beynon Thomas Papers
McGill University Archives
    Maude Abbott Papers and Diary
    John Clark-Murray Papers
    J.W. Dawson Papers
McGill University Rare Book Room
    Lady Roddick, Papers and Diaries
McCord Museum, Montreal
    Mrs Kate Hayter Reed, Diaries and Correspondence
Public Archives of Canada, Ottawa
    Lord and Lady Aberdeen Papers
    Sir Robert Borden Papers
    Mackenzie King Papers
    Sir Wilfrid Laurier Papers
    John A. Macdonald Papers
    William F. Maclean Papers
    Agnes Macphail Papers
    Arthur Meighen Papers

NCW of Canada, Papers and Correspondence, 1893–1919
Newton Rowell Papers
J.S. Woodsworth Papers
Queen's University, Kingston
Merrill Denison Papers
Archives of Saskatchewan
J.A. Calder Papers
Mrs S.V. (Zoa) Haight Papers
Violet M. MacNaughton Papers
W.R. Motherwell Papers
Walter Scott Papers
University of Toronto Archives
George M. Wrong, Public Papers and Correspondence
University of Toronto Rare Book Room
Flora Macdonald Denison, Papers, Scrapbooks, and Correspondence
United Church Archives, Toronto
Salem Bland Papers
Beatrice Brigden Papers
Albert Carman Papers
S.D. Chown Papers
William Lund Clark Papers
Victoria College Library, Toronto
Emily Stowe, Scrapbooks V and VI
Ontario Archives, Toronto
J.P. Whitney, Papers of the Prime Minister's Office
William Hearst, Papers of the Prime Minister's Office
Wilfrid Laurier University Archives
Emily Stowe, Private Papers, Scrapbooks III and IV
University of Waterloo, Special Collections
Louise Crummy McKinney, from the 'Famous Five' Alberta Women
Emily Murphy, Private Papers
Elizabeth Smith-Shortt, Papers, Correspondence, and Diary

PRINTED SOURCES

Albert College, Alexandra College, Papers re Founding, Syllabus
Alberta Women's Club, *Blue Book*, 1917
Alberta Women's Canadian Club, Calgary, 1913
Alberta Woman's Christian Temperance Union, Papers and Reports, 1910–16
Alliance Year Books, *The Prohibition Controversy*, 1884–5
Canadian Club of Montreal, *Addresses*, 1912, 1916
Canadian Women's Press Club, Ottawa Branch, Scrapbooks, Minute Books, 1916–30
– Edmonton Branch, *Club Women's Records*, 1916
Charity Organization Society of Montreal, *Annual Report*, 1901

Dominion Alliance, Ontario Branch, *Minutes*, Toronto, 1896, 1899
Dominion Woman's Christian Temperance Union, *Reports of Conventions*, 1899–1918
Dunham Ladies' College, Quebec, *Annual Calendar*, 1883–4
Hansard, *House of Commons Debates*; 1885 – debate on Macdonald's Franchise Act; 1916 – debate on William Pugsley's amendment
Imperial Order of Daughters of the Empire, *Souvenir*, 1916
International Council of Women, *Report*, June 1909, vols I and II
International Congress of Women, *Report*, vols I-VII, Ishbel Aberdeen, ed, 1899
Methodist Church: Department of Evangelism and Social Service, *Annual Reports*, 1906–18
Methodist Church, *Women and the Ministry*, 1921 Referendum
Methodist Church, *Deaconess Society*, Annual Reports, 1896–7; 1908–9
Methodists: World Ecumenical Conferences, 1881–1921
Montreal Child Welfare Exhibition, *Souvenir Handbook*, 1912
Montreal Directory of Women, *Report*, 1919
Montreal Ladies' Educational Society, *Reports*, 1871–82
Montreal Local Council of Women, *Reports*, 1897–1901
– Twenty-First Anniversary, *Reports for 1893–1915*
Montreal Parks and Playgrounds Association, *Annual Report*, 1904
Montreal Society for the Protection of Women and Children, *Minutes*, 1882–1918
Montreal Suffrage Association, *Minutes*, 1913–19
Montreal Woman's Christian Temperance Union, *Reports*, 1884–97
Montreal Women's Club, *Reports*, 1894–1901
National Council of Women of Canada, *Reports*, 1894–1918
Ontario Commission on Unemployment, *Report*, 1916
Ontario Woman's Christian Temperance Union, *Annual Reports*, 1878–1918
Ottawa Local Council of Women, *Minute Books*, 1896–9
Ottawa Women's Canadian Club, *Annual Reports*, 1912, 1915
Political Equality League of Manitoba, *Minutes*, 1912–14
Presbyterian General Assembly on Temperance and other Moral and Social Reforms, *Minutes*, 1907–10
Presbyterian Church in Canada: Board of Social Service and Evangelism, *Reports*, 1912, 1913, 1914
Presbyterian General Assembly, *Minutes*, 1913–18
Provincial Equal Franchise Board, Saskatchewan, *Minutes*, 1915–18
Quebec Woman's Christian Temperance Union, *Reports*, 1884–1905
Saskatchewan Grain Growers' Association, *Minutes and Reports*, 1912–17
– Women's Section, *Minutes*, 1914–18
Statutes of Ontario, re Married Women's Property Act, 1884
Toronto Collegiate Girls' Literary Society, *Minutes*, 1888–9
Toronto Ladies' Educational Association, *Reports*, 1874–5
Trades and Labour Congress, *Report* for the Thirteenth Annual Convention, 1914

University Women's Club of Ottawa, *Minutes*, 1910–16
University Women's Club of Winnipeg, *Civic Committee Report*, 1914
Woman's Institute of Stoney Creek, *Minutes*, 1897
Woman's Christian Temperance Union, Toronto District, *Reports*, 1905–19
Women's Institutes, British Columbia, *Annual Report*, 1914
Women's Institutes, Ontario, *Tweedsmuir Histories*
Women's War Register, Montreal, *Reports*, 1916–18
Young Women's Christian Association, Montreal, *Diet Dispensary*, 1884

NEWSPAPERS AND MAGAZINES

British Columbia Federationist, 1911–18
Canadian Labour Party Bulletin, Toronto, 3 April 1911
The Christian Guardian, Methodist Publication, 1890–1915
Dominion Illustrated Monthly, 1890–1
Farm and Ranch Review, 1915, 1916
Grain Growers' Guide, Winnipeg, 1911–17
Home Mission Pioneer, 1903–4, 1912, 1914
Industrial Banner, Hamilton, 1910–18
Labour Gazette, April 1913
McGill Daily, 1911–19
McGill Fortnightly, 1892–8
McGill Martlett, 1908–11
McGill News, miscellaneous articles re Carrie Derick
McGill Outlook, 1899–1906
McGill Scrapbooks, volumes I–III, 1853–1921
McGill University Magazine, miscellaneous articles
Methodist Magazine and Review, 1875–1906
Montreal Gazette, 1892, 1897, 1914–17
Montreal Herald, 1912–17
Montreal Star, 1912, 1933
Montreal Witness, 1909–13
Old McGill, 1898–1916
Presbyterian Witness, Halifax, 1913–16
Sunset of Bon Echo, edited by Flora Macdonald Denison, 1916, 1919
Toronto Globe, 1910–17
Toronto News, 1911
Toronto World, 1909–17
Vancouver Sun, 1913
Victoria Times, 1913–17
Winnipeg Free Press, 1911–17
Winnipeg Voice, 1909–17
Wives and Daughters, Oct. 1890
Woman's Century, official organ of NCW, 1916
Women's Patriotic Journal, St Catharines, Nov. 1914
The Young Women of Canada, 1910–11

BOOKS

Aberdeen, Lord and Lady *We Twa*, volume II. London: W. Collins Sons and Co 1925

Allen, Grant *The Woman Who Did*. Boston: Roberts Bros 1895

Atkinson, D.T. *Social Travesties and What They Cost*. New York: Vail-Ballou Co 1916

Austin, B.F., ed *The Prohibition Leaders of America*. St Thomas: Alma College 1895

– *Woman; her Character, Culture and Calling*. Ontario: Book and Bible House 1890

Bain, Mildred *Horace Traubel*. New York: Albert-Charles Boni 1913

Barry, Lily E.F. *In the Paths of Peace*. Montreal: Canada Engraving and Litho Co 1901

Bengough, J.W. *Bengough's Chalk-Talks*. Toronto: Musson Book Co 1922

Beynon, Francis M. *Aleta Dey*. Toronto: Thomas Allen 1919

Binnie-Clark, Georgina *Wheat and Woman*. Toronto: Bell and Cockburn 1914; reprint, University of Toronto Press 1979

Bland, Salem G. *James Henderson, D.D.* Toronto: McClelland and Stewart 1926

Blease, W. Lyon *The Emancipation of English Women*. London: Constable and Co 1910

Burke, Dr Richard Maurice *Cosmic Consciousness*. Philadelphia: Innes and Sons 1910

Burry, Beatrice (Pullen) *From Halifax to Vancouver*. London: Mills and Boon 1912

Cameron, Agnes Dean *The New North*. London: D. Appleton and Co 1912

Carpenter, Edward *Love's Coming of Age*. New York: Mitchell Kennerley 1911

Chesser, Elizabeth Sloan *Woman, Marriage, and Motherhood*. London: Cassell and Co 1913

Chown, Alice A. *The Stairway*. Boston: Cornhill Co 1921

Clark, William Lund *Our Sons*. Ontario: W.L. Clark 1914

Committee of Fifteen *The Social Evil: With Special Reference to Conditions in the City of New York*. New York 1902

Connor, Ralph *The Friendly Four and Other Stories*. New York: George H. Doran Co 1926

Cotes, Sarah Jeannette (Duncan) *A Daughter of Today*. New York: D. Appleton and Co 1894

– *The Imperialist*. Toronto: McClelland and Stewart 1904

Cran, Mrs George *A Woman in Canada*. Toronto: Musson Book Co 1910

Denison, Flora Macdonald *Mary Melville: The Psychic*. Toronto: Austin Publishing Co 1900

Drake, Emma F. Angell *What a Young Wife Ought to Know*. London: Vir Publishing Co 1901

Dougall, Lily *The Madonna of a Day*. London: Richard Bentley and Son 1896

Ferguson, Emily *Open Trails*. Toronto: J.M. Dent and Sons 1920

– *Janey Canuck in the West*. Toronto: Wayfarers' Library 1917

Hale, Beatrice Forbes-Robertson *What Women Want*. New York: Frederick A. Stokes Co 1914

Hale, Katherine *Canadian Cities of Romance*. Toronto: McClelland and Stewart 1933

Hall, Mrs Cecil *A Lady's Life on a Farm in Manitoba*. London: W.H. Allen and Co 1884

Herring, Francis E. *Nan and Other Pioneer Women of the West*. London: Francis Griffiths 1913

Hind, E. Cora *My Travels and Findings*. Toronto: Macmillan Company of Canada 1939

Hopkins, Castell *The Province of Ontario in the War*. Toronto: Warwick Bros and Rutler 1919

Hunter, Rev W.J. *Manhood, Wrecked and Rescued*. Toronto: William Briggs 1894

Knox, Ellen M. *The Girl of the New Day*. Toronto: McClelland and Stewart 1919

Labour Department *Legal Status of Women in Canada*. Ottawa: F.A. Acland 1924

Langton, Anne *A Gentlewoman in Upper Canada*. Toronto: Clarke, Irwin and Co 1950

McClung, Nellie *Sowing Seeds in Danny*. Toronto: William Briggs 1912
- *The Second Chance*. Toronto: William Briggs 1914
- *In Times Like These*. Toronto: McLeod and Allen 1915
- *The Next of Kin*. Toronto: Thomas Allen 1917
- *Purple Springs*. New York: Houghton Mifflin Co 1922
- *When Christmas Crossed the Peace*. Toronto: Thomas Allen 1923
- *Painted Fires*. Toronto: Thomas Allen 1925
- *All We Like Sheep*. Toronto: Thomas Allen 1926
- *Be Good to Yourself*. Toronto: Thomas Allen 1930
- *Flowers for the Living*. Toronto: Thomas Allen 1931
- *Clearing in the West*. Toronto: Thomas Allen 1935
- *The Stream Runs Fast*. Toronto: Thomas Allen 1945

McCrimmon, A.L. *The Woman Movement*. Chicago: Griffith and Rowland Press 1915

MacMurchy, Marjory *The Woman – Bless Her*. Toronto: S.B. Grundy 1916

MacPhail, Andrew *The Master's Wife*. Montreal: Gnaedinger Printing Co 1939
- *Essays in Fallacy*. London: Longmans, Green and Co 1910

Massey, Alice Vincent *Occupations for Trained Women in Canada*. Toronto: J.M. Dent and Sons 1920

Mayreder, Rosa *A Survey of the Woman Problem*. London: William Heinemann 1913

Mitchell, E.B. *In Western Canada Before the War*. London: John Murray 1915

Moodie, Susannah *Life in the Backwoods*. New York: John W. Lovell Co 1887

Morgan, Henry James, ed *Types of Canadian Women*. Toronto: William Briggs 1903

Morris, Elizabeth *An English Woman in the Canadian West*. London: Simpkin Marshall 1913

Murphy, Emily *Seeds of Pine*. Toronto: Hodder and Stoughton 1914

– *The Black Candle*. Toronto: Thomas Allen 1922

National Council of Women of Canada *Women of Canada: Their Life and Their Work*, Ishbel Aberdeen, ed, Paris International Exhibition, 1900

Raymond, A. Pauline *Gathered Sheaves from the National Council of Women*. New Brunswick: J. and A. McMillan 1921

Re-Bartlett, Lucy *Sex and Sanctity*. New York: Longmans, Green and Co 1912

– *The Coming Order*. New York: Longmans, Green and Co 1911

Reid, Helen R.Y. *A Social Study Along Health Lines*. Montreal 1920

Richardson, Benjamin Ward *Public School Temperance*. Toronto: Grip Publishing and Printing 1887

Ridley, Hilda M. *The Post-War Woman*. Toronto: Ryerson Press 1941

Ross, Alexander Milton *Memoirs of a Reformer*. Toronto: Hunter, Rose and Co 1893

Roy, Gabrielle *The Tin Flute*. New York: Reynal and Hitchcock 1947

Saleeby, C.W. *Woman and Womanhood*. London: William Heinemann 1912

Salverson, Laura Goodman *The Viking Heart*. Toronto: McClelland and Stewart 1923

– *When Sparrows Fall*. Toronto: Thomas Allen 1925

Saywell, J.T., ed *Lady Aberdeen's Canadian Journal*. Toronto: Champlain Society 1960

Schirmacher, Dr Kaethe *The Modern Woman's Rights Movement*. New York: Macmillan Co 1912

Schreiner, Olive *Woman and Labor*. New York: Frederick A. Stokes 1911

Schuster, Edgar *Eugenics*. London: Collins' Press 1912

Seton-Thompson, Grace *A Woman Tenderfoot*. New York: Doubleday, Page, and Co 1900

Smith, Minnie *Is It Just?*. Toronto: William Briggs 1911

Spence, F.S. *The Facts of the Case: Royal Commission on the Liquor Traffic*. Toronto: Newton and Treloar 1896

Social Service Congress of Canada *Report of Proceedings and Addresses*. Toronto: Ontario Press 1914

Strange, Kathleen *With the West in Her Eyes*. New York: Dodge Publishing Co 1937

Swiney, Frances *The Awakening of Women OR Woman's Part in Evolution*. London: William Reeves 1899

Sykes, Ella C. *A Home-Help in Canada*. London: Smith, Elder, and Co 1912

Symonds, Herbert *A Memoir*, Compiled by Friends. Montreal: Renauf Publishing Co 1921

Traubel, Horace, ed *In Re Walt Whitman*. Philadelphia: David McKay 1893

– *With Walt Whitman in Camden*. New York: D. Appleton and Co 1908

Webster, Rev Thomas *Woman, Man's Equal*. Cincinnati: Hitchcock and Walder 1873

Weaver, Emily P. *The Canadian Woman's Annual and Social Service Directory*. Toronto: McClelland, Goodchild, and Stewart 1915
Whyte, John M. *Nuggets of Gold for Temperance Campaigns*. Toronto: William Briggs 1898
Willard, Frances *Woman and Temperance*. Connecticut: Park Publishing Co 1883
– *Woman in the Pulpit*. Boston: D. Lothrop and Co 1888
– *My Happy Half-Century*. London: Ward, Lock, and Bowder 1895
Williams, Frances Fenwick *A Soul on Fire*. New York: John Lane Co 1915
Women's Canadian Club *Women of Red River to 1873*. Winnipeg: Butman Bros 1923
Wood-Allen, Mary *What a Young Woman Ought to Know*. London: Vir Publishing Co 1898
Woodsworth, James *Thirty Years in the Canadian North-West*. Toronto: McClelland, Goodchild, and Stewart 1917
Woodsworth, J.S. *Strangers Within Our Gates*. Canada: Frederick Clarke Stephenson 1909; reprint, University of Toronto Press 1972, introduction by Marilyn Barber
– *My Neighbor*. Toronto: University of Toronto Press reprint 1972
Youmans, Letitia *Campaign Echoes*. Toronto: William Briggs 1893

ARTICLES

Armitage, May L. 'The First Woman Magistrate in Canada.' *Maclean's Magazine*, Oct. 1916
– 'Mrs Nellie McClung.' *Maclean's Magazine*, July 1915
Blackburn, Stephen 'An Estimate of Canadian Women.' *Canadian Magazine*, Toronto 1895
Cartwright, M. 'A College for Women.' *University of Toronto Monthly*, Nov. 1909
Charlesworthy, Hector W. 'The Canadian Girl.' *Canadian Magazine*, Toronto 1893
Colquhoun, Ethel 'Feminism and Education.' *McGill University Magazine*, vol XII, 1913
Cox, Caroline O. 'Play for the People.' *McGill University Magazine*, vol VII, 1908
Cummings, Mrs Willoughby 'Woman's Sphere.' *Canadian Magazine*, 1901
Dale, Dorothea 'The Millionth Woman.' *Canadian Magazine*, 1896
Denison, Flora Macdonald 'Mrs Pankhurst – Premier Hearst.' *Sunset of Bon Echo*, 1916
– 'The Unemployed and Zero Weather.' Unpublished
Derick, Carrie 'Variation and Heredity in Plants.' *McGill University Magazine*, December 1903
Dixon, F.J. 'Let the Women Vote.' *Grain Growers' Guide*, 26 May 1913
Edgar, Maude C. 'The Higher Education of Women.' *University of Toronto Monthly*, May 1908
Harvie, L.J. 'Fallen Women.' Ontario WCTU Report, 1870

Hawkes, Arthur 'Why I am a Suffragette.' *Canadian Magazine*, 1909
Huestis, Mary J. 'The Women Workers of Canada.' *Scientific American*, 12 Jan. 1918
Lambert, Norman 'A Joan of the West.' *Canadian Magazine*, 1915
Leacock, Stephen 'The Woman Question.' *Maclean's Magazine*, Oct. 1915
Leathes, Sonia 'Votes for Women.' *McGill University Magazine*, Feb. 1914
Lefroy, A.H.F. 'Should Canadian Women Have the Parliamentary Vote?' *Queen's Quarterly*, vol xxi, 1913
Macbeth, Madge 'Canadian Women in the Professions.' *Maclean's Magazine*, March 1915; May 1915
McClung, Nellie 'Speaking of Women.' *Maclean's Magazine*, May 1916
– 'What Will They do With It?' *Maclean's Magazine*, July 1916
MacDonald, I.L. 'The Status of Women in the Province of Quebec.' *McGill University Publications*, series 6, #1–17, 1920
Machar, Agnes M. 'Higher Education for Women.' *Canadian Monthly*, Toronto 1875
Maclellan, W.E. 'Women and Votes.' *Dalhousie Review*, vol I, 1922
MacMurchy, Marjorie 'Women of To-day and To-morrow.' *Canadian Magazine*, 1919
MacNaughton, Prof R.E. 'A Plea for Woman Suffrage in Canada.' *Canadian Magazine*, 1907
Macphail, Andrew 'On Certain Aspects of Feminism.' *McGill University Magazine*, Feb. 1914
– 'Women in Democracy.' *McGill University Magazine*, Feb. 1920
Murphy, Emily F. 'What Janey Thinks of Nellie.' *Maclean's Magazine*, Sept. 1921
– 'About Marriage' and other articles in the *National Monthly of Canada*, 1902–4
Parker, Annie 'Women in Nation Building,' in B.F. Austin, ed, *Woman; Her Character, Culture and Calling*, 1890
Perry, Anne Anderson 'Is Women's Suffrage a Fizzle?' *Maclean's Magazine*, Feb. 1928
Ridley, Hilda 'Love and Labour.' *Canadian Magazine*, 1912
Skelton, Isabel 'Canadian Women and the Suffrage.' *Canadian Magazine*, 1913
Smith, Goldwin 'Female Suffrage.' *Canadian Monthly*, 1874
– 'The Woman's Rights Movement.' *Canadian Monthly*, 1872
Vaughan, W. 'Woman Suffrage To-Day,' *McGill University Magazine*, Dec. 1916
Walton, F.P. 'Divorce in Canada and the United States: A Contrast.' *McGill University Magazine*, vol ix, 1910
Williams, Frank H. 'Cora Hind.' *Maclean's Magazine*, June 1935
Wrong, G.M. 'A College for Women.' *University of Toronto Monthly*, Nov. 1909

PAMPHLETS

Bryce, Peter H. *The Ethical Problems Underlying the Social Evil*. Toronto 1914
Counter, Charles A. *Woman's Rights*. Kingston 1882

Crawford, Mary E. *Legal Status of Women in Manitoba*. Political Equality
League of Manitoba 1913

Edwards, Henrietta Muir *Legal Status of Canadian Women*. National Council of
Women 1908

Eliot, Dr Charles W. *The Double Standard of Morals and the Social Diseases*.
Department of Temperance and Moral Reform of the Methodist Church,
Toronto, undated

Gullen, A. (Stowe) *A Brief History of the Ontario Medical College for Women*.
Toronto 1906

Hughes, James L. *Equal Suffrage*. Toronto: William Briggs 1895

Kauffman, Reginald Wright *The Girl That Goes Wrong*. Department of Temperance and Moral Reform of Methodist Church, undated

Leathes, Sonia *What Equal Suffrage Has Accomplished*. Toronto 1910

MacGill, Helen Gregory *Daughters, Wives, and Mothers in British Columbia:
Some Laws Regarding Them*. British Columbia: Moore Printing Co 1913

Methodist Church *Principles, Problems, Programme in Moral and Social Reforms*.
Department of Temperance and Moral Reform, 1910–11

Non-Partisan League *Six Reasons Why You Should Vote for Mrs S.V. Haight*.
1917

Parkman, Francis *Some of the Reasons Against Woman Suffrage*. U.S.A. 1912

Scott, Jean Thompson *The Conditions of Female Labour in Ontario*. Toronto
University Studies in Political Science 1892

Shearer, Rev J.G., and Moore, T.A. *Canada's War on the White Slave Traffic*.
Department of Temperance and Moral Reform of Methodist Church,
undated

Social Service Council of Canada *Moral Conditions Among Our Soldiers Overseas*. Toronto c 1918

Squire, John *Admission of Women to the University of Toronto and University
College*. University of Toronto Press 1924

Watt, D.A. *Moral Legislation: A Statement Prepared for the Information of the
Senate*. 1890

Weir, Mr Recorder *The Social Evil: Toleration Condemned*. Presbyterian Church
in Canada, Board of Moral and Social Reform and Evangelism, Montreal
1909

Wilson, Sir Daniel *Coeducation – a letter to the Hon. G.W. Ross*. Toronto:
Hunter, Rose and Co 1884

Bibliographical Essay

The standard work on the Canadian woman suffrage movement is Catherine Cleverdon's *The Woman Suffrage Movement in Canada*, first published in 1950 by University of Toronto Press and recently (1974) reprinted with an excellent introduction by Ramsay Cook. Cleverdon's study is a thorough and scholarly narrative of incidents and events at both the federal and provincial levels. Similar descriptive narratives have been written about the American movement by Eleanor Flexner (*Century of Struggle: The Woman's Rights Movement in the United States*, Massachusetts: Belknap Press 1968), the English movement by Constance Rover (*Woman's Suffrage and Party Politics in Britain, 1866–1914*, Toronto: University of Toronto Press 1967) and the New Zealand movement by Patricia Grimshaw (*Women's Suffrage in New Zealand*, Auckland: Auckland University Press 1972).

American historians have led the way in producing major interpretive studies of the movement's ideology. In 1965 Aileen Kraditor wrote *The Ideas of the Woman Suffrage Movement, 1890–1920* (New York: Columbia University Press). This was followed in 1967 by Alan P. Grimes, *The Puritan Ethic and Woman Suffrage* (New York: Oxford University Press) and in 1969 by William O'Neill, *Everyone was Brave: a History of Feminism in America* (Chicago: Quadrangle Books). All three studies recognized the moderate nature of the suffragists' social programme and all three attributed it to the women's class and race allegiances.

In a path-breaking article in *Feminist Studies* (Fall 1975) entitled 'The Radicalism of the Woman Suffrage Movement: Notes Toward the Reconstruction of Nineteenth-Century Feminism,' Ellen du Bois insisted upon assessing the suffragists' activities in terms of their own times. She distinguished between 'sphere' and 'role' and noted how difficult it was for women to move from the 'domestic' to the 'public' sphere. The fact that the majority were content to work within traditional female role-models she does not deny. These ideas have been expanded in her *Feminism and Suffrage: The Emergence of an Independent Woman's Movement in America, 1848–1869* (Ithaca: Cornell University Press 1978). Linda Gordon's thorough investigation of the American birth control movement fits into this tradition since she interprets the feminists' rejection of artificial birth control devices and endorsement of abstinence as the only option available to them because of the pressures of public opinion (*Woman's Body; Woman's Right: a History of Birth Control in America*, Harmondsworth, Middlesex: Penguin 1977).

Some recent Canadian writings have opened up new areas of debate. Three articles (by Wayne Roberts, Deborah Gorham, and Veronica Strong-Boag) in *A Not Unreasonable Claim: Women and Reform in Canada, 1880's–1920's* (edited by Linda Kealey; Toronto: The Women's Press 1979) examine the ideological strengths and weaknesses of the Canadian movement. Roberts and Strong-Boag point out how the professionalism of the majority led them into select but secure positions, and distracted them from feminist issues.

Important general interpretations of the larger reform movement are Richard Hofstadter, *The Age of Reform* (New York: Vintage Books 1955) and Robert Wiebe, *The Search for Order* (New York: Hill and Wang 1967). Hofstadter introduced the now much-discredited concept of 'status anxiety' to explain reform behaviour. Wiebe demonstrated the wide support for reform in the business community and the consequent infatuation with bureaucratic models. Paul Boyer's recent *Urban Masses and Moral Order in America, 1820–1920* (Cambridge, Massachusetts: Harvard University Press 1978) offers a broader interpretation of progressivism. He identifies two strands of thought which he labels 'negative' and 'positive' environmentalism depending upon the methods adopted. His reformers show some signs of class bias but only one communal bond incorporates the many faces of progressivism, according to Boyer – 'an infinite capacity for moral indignation.'

The intellectual climate in which the progressives operated is set out in Melvin Richter, *The Politics of Conscience: T.H. Green and his Age* (London: Weidenfeld and Nicolson 1964). Christopher Lasch in *The New Radicalism in America: The Intellectual as a Social Type* (New York: Alfred A. Knopf 1965) describes the particular pressures affecting the intelligentsia. Attempts by Canadian historians to examine the general reform ethos are almost nonexistent. W.L. Morton's classic, *The Progressive Party in Canada* (Toronto: University of Toronto Press 1950), stands on its own in this respect.

Particular strands of the reform movement have attracted more attention. Temperance, for example, has been thoroughly investigated. The initial studies were once again American: James H. Timberlake, *Prohibition and the Progressive Movement, 1900–1920* (Cambridge, Massachusetts: Harvard University Press 1963) and Joseph R. Gusfield, *Symbolic Crusade: Status Politics and the American Temperance Movement* (Urbana: University of Illinois Press 1963). See also Gusfield, 'Social Structure and Moral Reform: A Study of the Woman's Christian Temperance Union,' *American Journal of Sociology*, Nov. 1955–6. Janet Zollinger Giele's thesis, 'Social Change in the Feminine Role: A Comparison of Woman's Suffrage and Woman's Temperance' (PHD, Radcliffe College 1961) has been the only attempt to compare and contrast the ideas of temperance women and suffragists.

Most of Canada's studies of the temperance movement are still in thesis form: Albert J. Hiebert, 'Prohibition in British Columbia' (MA, Simon Fraser 1969); Robert Irwin Maclean, 'A "Most Effectual" Remedy: Temperance and Prohibition in Alberta, 1875–1915' (MA, University of Calgary 1969); John H. Thompson, 'The Prohibition Question in Manitoba' (MA, University of Manitoba 1969); Malcolm Graeme Decarie, 'The Prohibition Movement in Ontario, 1894–1916' (PHD, Queen's University 1972). The exceptions are Gerald Hallowell's *Prohibition in Ontario, 1919–1923* (Toronto: Ontario Historical Society 1974), John H. Thompson's article, 'The Beginning of Our Regeneration: The Great War and Western Canadian Reform Movements' (Canadian Historical Association, *Historical Papers*, 1972) and Wendy Mitchinson's recent contribution to Linda Kealey's collection, entitled 'The W.C.T.U: "For God, Home and Native Land": A Study in Nineteenth-Century Feminism.'

Richard Allen has the distinction of producing the most comprehensive study of the religious side of reform. His 1968 article in *Canadian Historical Review*, 'The Social Gospel and the Reform Tradition in Canada,' and his book, *The Social Passion: Religion and Social Reform in Canada, 1914–1928* (Toronto: University of Toronto Press 1971) investigate the religious inspiration which motivated many of Canada's reformers.

The secular reform movement must be broken down into its several segments since no one as yet has treated it as a single phenomenon (Boyer might be considered an exception here). R.J.W. Selleck produced the classic study of late-nineteenth- and early-twentieth-century educational reform in *The New Education, 1870–1914* (London: Isaac Putnam and Sons 1968). Some Canadians have taken up particular aspects of this movement: Bruce N. Carter, 'James L. Hughes and the Gospel of Education' (Doctor of Education, University of Toronto 1966); Robert Miles Stamp, 'The Campaign for Technical Education in Ontario, 1876–1914' (PHD, University of Western Ontario 1970); Alison Prentice, *The School Promoters: Education and Social Class in Mid-Nineteenth Century Upper Canada* (Toronto: McClelland and Stewart 1971).

The fourth section in Neil Sutherland, *Children in English-Canadian Society: Framing the Twentieth-Century Consensus* (Toronto: University of Toronto Press 1976) deals specifically with the 'New Education' in Canada but the book goes far beyond this subject. Sutherland's challenging presentation of changing attitudes towards children, child welfare, juvenile delinquency, and education comes closest to feeling the pulse of the population in this period in Canada. See also Sutherland, '"To Create a Strong and Healthy Race": School Children in the Public Health Movement,' *History of Education Quarterly*, Fall 1972, and Susan Houston, 'Victorian Origins of Juvenile Delinquency: A Canadian Experience' in the same volume. Terrence R. Morrison's thesis, 'The Child and Urban Social Reform in Late Nineteenth-Century Ontario, 1875–1900' (PHD, University of Toronto 1970), part of which has been reproduced in '"Their Proper Sphere": Feminism, The Family, and Child-Centered Social Reform in Ontario, 1875–1900,' *Ontario History*, March and June 1976, examines attitudes towards children in relation to their impact on attitudes towards women, making it perhaps the most valuable work for students of the woman's movement.

The best study of the social purity crusade is David J. Pivar, 'The New Abolitionism: the Quest for Social Purity, 1876–1900' (PHD, University of Pennsylvania 1965), now a book, *Purity Crusade: Sexual Morality and Social Order, 1868–1900* (Westport, Connecticut: Greenwood Press 1973).

The most complete account of hereditarian thought in the period, as held by the reformers, is Donald K. Pickens, *Eugenics and the Progressives* (Nashville: Vanderbilt University Press 1968). Finally, two Canadian historians have provided excellent insights into the municipal reform movement in Canada: Paul Rutherford, 'Tomorrow's Metropolis: The Urban Reform Movement in Canada, 1880–1920,' *Canadian Historical Papers*, 1971, and John C. Weaver, 'The Meaning of Municipal Reform: Toronto, 1895,' *Ontario History*, June 1974.

Index

The Social History of Canada

General Editors:
Michael Bliss 1971–7
H.V. Nelles 1978–

#1